Western Lands and Waters Series
XVII

The Frontier World of
FORT GRIFFIN

The Life and Death
of a Western Town

by
Charles M. Robinson III

THE ARTHUR H. CLARK COMPANY
Spokane, Washington   1992

To Perla and Rita

Contents

Illustrations

Acknowledgements

Many individuals and organizations helped in this project and I wish to acknowledge their efforts.

The late C.L. Sonnichsen of Tucson, Arizona, read the chapters on the Shackelford County Vigilance Committee, the Larn Affair and the Brock Case. He not only made comments and offered suggestions from a historical point of view, but gave valuable editorial help as well. Mr. Sonnichsen was a very busy man, and the amount of time he gave to this project is deeply appreciated.

Dean Lawrence Clayton, College of Arts and Sciences, Hardin-Simmons University, Abilene, Texas, read the above chapters and offered valuable insights on his wife's grandfather, John Chadbourne Irwin. He also provided me with copies of notes for a book he had once planned to write, and managed to secure a photograph of Irwin. I am grateful for all his help and encouragement.

Thanks also to Joan Farmer, archivist, and Elsa Turner, volunteer, Old Jail Art Center and Archive, Albany, Texas. They spent most of one afternoon and all of the following day going over historical information and old traditions of Shackelford County, and their conversation was as valuable as the written material. Mrs. Farmer also made several phone calls to my home to inquire whether I needed specific photographs, as well as an even greater contribution listed below.

Mrs. J.C. Putnam welcomed me, a total stranger, into her home, which was designed, built and occupied by John Larn. She and her daughter showed me through the house, told me everything they knew about it, and gave me free run of the grounds.

Doris Byars, Scurry County Museum, Snyder, Texas, made several long-distance calls to help me run down photographs of the Mooar brothers.

Mrs. Claire Kuehn, librarian, Panhandle-Plains Historical Society, Canyon, provided me with copies of numerous articles and papers over a one-year period.

Thanks to Ralph Elder and the staff of the Eugene C. Barker Texas History Center, University of Texas, Austin, for all their efforts on my behalf, particularly at a time when they were shorthanded.

James L. Haley of Austin offered valuable suggestions and encouragement, and most importantly, his friendship.

Special thanks to the staff at the San Benito Public Library, Noemi Garza, director; Sandra Flores, assistant director; Rosie Mares, Interlibrary Loan clerk, and all the others for extraordinary efforts in securing research material, calling me when it came in, and having a pot of coffee and sweet rolls when I arrived. This was done purely out of friendship and belief in what I was doing. No words can describe the support they have been.

Hardin-Simmons University Library, Abilene, Joe Dahlstrom, director of University Libraries, and the estate of Ben O. Grant provided permission to quote from Grant's pioneering thesis, "The Early History of Shackelford County." I was also given access to the valuable J.R. Webb Papers, located in the Rupert N. Richardson Research Center in the library.

Texas Tech University Library gave clearance to quote from Jimmy Skaggs' thesis, "The Great Western Cattle Trail to Dodge City, Kansas."

The late Wayne Gard offered leads on researching the Vigilance Committee, the buffalo hunt and the cattle drives.

Thanks also to Lester Galbreath, park superintendent and staff, Texas Department of Parks and Wildlife, Fort Griffin State Historical Park; Bobbie Cox, district clerk of Shackelford County, Albany; Robert B. Dunkin, Rosa M. Muñoz, Frank W. Sanchez, Ernest Taubert and L. Nathan Winters for their friendship and encouragement; to Henry Krausse, chairman of the Cameron County Historical Commission for his backing; to Mrs. Menton Murray Sr., member of the board of the Texas State Historical Association and my eighth grade history teacher; and to Tol Boswell Jr. and Sam Penn Boswell, L.T. Boswell Ford-SAAB, for helping arrange transportation.

Finally, to my wife, Perla, for proofreading everything and for tolerating piles of books and files on the dining room table and living room floor; to my daughter, Rita, for putting up with a long and (to her) often boring drive to Albany, and for understanding that there were times I couldn't take her somewhere or play a game; and to my mother, Rosalyn C. Robinson.

The events in this book are as true as anything can be after one hundred years. Every effort has been made to sort out legends and resolve conflicting accounts. However, it is not the last word. New information comes to light from time to time. Two years after this project started, after I thought I was finished, the official papers on the Larn affair came to light. A citizen of Shackelford County ran across them, folded and stuck into a book, after being lost for more than a century. This citizen provided photocopies to Joan Farmer, who passed them on to me. Even this record is not complete—before Mrs. Farmer got them, some names had been carefully removed from the depositions. Still, these papers change everything previously written on the arrest and death of John Larn.

Now that the Larn files have been recovered, it is reasonable to assume other information may also reappear. Perhaps we will one day learn what really happened during Doc Holliday's stay in the Flat, or the truth about Lottie Deno.

Whatever happens, and regardless of who helped with this project, I alone am responsible for the final narrative and conclusions drawn.

San Benito, Texas
July 1991

A Word About Spelling

Most people on the frontier were remarkably literate, but their spelling left much to be desired. Words and names were often spelled phonetically.

When quoting directly from period sources, I have preserved the original spelling and punctuation. However, when proper names are given outside of direct quotes I have used the most common spelling of the period for the sake of uniformity. For example, any Irishman worthy of the Green would insist on "Shaughnessy." Yet, I have spelled it "Shannessy" throughout, since that was the spelling most commonly encountered in Fort Griffin. Likewise, although "Matthews" is used in *Interwoven*, I have spelled it "Mathews," as that is the form I have most commonly encountered.

Given names present another problem, as some people have been called by two or three different names. In one or two cases, they might have used different names at different times. But by and large, the conflicts occur in the recollections of pioneers, some in their nineties, who were trying to recall events which happened sixty years earlier. Thus Johnny Shannessy and John William Poe (the forms used here), are called Dick Shannessy and Joe Poe in some works.

All place names use the modern spelling except in direct quotes. In cases where a name has changed in the last century (i.e. Fort Concho to San Angelo, Indian Territory to Oklahoma), the original name is used for the sake of consistency.

Prologue: The Flat

U.S. Highway 283 crosses the Red River from Oklahoma into Texas in Wilbarger County, not far west of Wichita Falls. From there, it runs over rolling prairies, with grass, scrub trees and rocks, broken here and there by solitary round hills rising up from the plains. It is good cattle country, watered by occasional rivers and creeks which flood or trickle depending on the season of the year.

Looking on the current road map published by the Texas Department of Highways and Public Transportation, you can follow 283 in a more or less southerly direction, through Baylor and Throckmorton counties and into Shackelford County. Just inside Shackelford, the highway crosses the Clear Fork of the Brazos River, and (according to the map) passes through a little town called Fort Griffin.

That spot on the map is all of the town you will see. There is no Fort Griffin.

Instead, there are a couple of wood frame farm houses, a stock watering pool, tall, thick trees such as line watercourses in this part of the country, a couple of dirt tracks and a ruined stone building. A few hundred yards farther, a sign points to Fort Griffin State Historical Park, on either side of the highway. It denotes the ruins of a military post left over from the Indian Wars, not a town.

Is the map wrong?

Technically, perhaps.

But in 1878, the town of Fort Griffin was the economic center of the region. Located on the east-west stage run, it was the biggest concern between Fort Worth and El Paso. On the north-south line of the cattle trails, it was the only major settlement between San Antonio and Dodge City. By frontier standards, it was busy and rich. And together with Dodge City, Deadwood and Tombstone, it was one of the four toughest towns the West ever saw.

Fort Griffin had its origins in the humdrum days of the 1850s, when most activity was in east and central Texas and along the Mexican border. Still, some stockmen started moving into the Clear Fork Valley, and these people needed military protection. The military presence was more preventive than active. While there were sporadic raids, the Indians were quiet in comparison to how they would be later, and the Army was not trained or equipped to chase them down anyway. All this changed during the War Between the States. With troops off fighting in Virginia and the frontier protected by an overworked, undermanned militia, the Indians swept through the settlements, pushing the line of defense a hundred miles east of where it had been a few years previously. Thus, after the war ended in the east, the federal government established a new line of military posts, garrisoned by battle-hardened professionals more than ready to end the Indian threat for good. One of these posts was Fort Griffin.

It was only natural for people to settle under the protection of the army. But it wasn't until the Indians had been permanently subdued that the town of Fort Griffin really got moving. With the plains cleared of hostile tribes, buffalo hunters were free to slaughter the great southern herd which blanketed west Texas. These people and their supporting cast—hunt outfitters, gamblers, saloonkeepers and ladies of easy virtue—were the first real settlers in Fort Griffin. They occupied a flat stretch of ground about half a mile wide, between the fort on Government Hill and the Clear Fork. Consequently, the town of Fort Griffin came to be known as the Flat. It was also called Hide Town, since the main industry was buffalo hides.

As the buffalo were hunted out, the cowboys came. The Great Western Trail ran through Fort Griffin and straight upcountry to Dodge City. For awhile, this ramshackle collection of tents and shacks on the Clear Fork was the transit center for Texas, threatening even Fort Worth.

The Flat ran day and night. Having a full-time population of a few hundred, offset by several thousand transient parasites, it was no place for a tenderfoot, or a man who couldn't handle himself. Nothing has yet equalled the biblical Sodom, but Fort Griffin certainly tried. If you were slick with cards or fast with a gun, the Flat was the Promised Land.

This kind of environment was bound to produce some kind of side effect, generally permanent for the person affected. The trees along the Clear Fork were good and solid, strong enough to support two hundred pounds or so of dead weight at the end of a rope. And according to the old newspaper accounts, the trees were often decorated with former citizens and transients. The Clear Fork itself was sufficient to sink a body, and by the time it was found, it was so badly decomposed it couldn't be recognized. When a body doesn't have a name, there is no motive, and consequently, no suspect. The plains surrounding Griffin were wide and lonely and hid their share of secrets as well.

In spite of it all, Fort Griffin deserved better than its ultimate oblivion. There were decent people in town, hard working and industrious. People attended church meetings. They went on picnics. They threw Christmas parties for children. Men hunted and fished, and ladies made their social rounds. As the economy shifted, so did the far-sighted business community. The merchant princes of Fort Griffin, such as they were, were not willing to pull up stakes and leave simply because the easy money had played out. They wanted their Flat to live, and they wanted to help make it live. It wasn't their fault Fort Griffin ultimately failed. It was a series of economic disasters in rapid succession. In those days, there was no state or federal aid to keep a town afloat when it had outlived its usefulness. When a town could no longer function, it simply died. Fort Griffin died.

There may be nothing left of the Flat itself but a few broken walls and foundations, and the vague trace of Griffin Avenue, but the citizens of Shackelford County keep it alive with their annual Fort Griffin Fandangle each June. The great families owe their existence to the Flat, and the average citizen feels a great pride in the pioneer heritage. Go to a coffee shop at the county seat in Albany and mention the Flat. Someone will start talking.

Fort Griffin was everything you could imagine about the west.

So maybe the highway department is wrong to keep it on the map. But may it never correct the error.

1

The Post on the
Clear Fork

When the Republic of Texas was annexed to the
United States in 1845, the American government
assumed responsibility for frontier defense. The most
immediate problem was Mexico, since annexation led
to war with that country. But with the end of the
Mexican War, the U.S. found itslf in a protracted
conflict with the Plains Indian tribes. These sporadic
wars dated back to colonial times, and neither settler
nor Indian showed any interest in ending them.

To control the situation, the federal government
erected a chain of forts down the western edge of the
frontier. The northern anchor of this chain was Fort
Worth on the Trinity River. From there, it ran southwest to Fort Duncan on the Rio Grande. This was
expected not only to contain the plains tribes in the
west, particularly the Kiowas and Comanches, but the
settlers in the east as well.

But the government had failed to reckon with the
settlers. Ninety years earlier, they had pushed beyond
the British line of containment in Appalachia. Now, as
the 1850s dawned, they pushed beyond the American
line. By 1852, the first forts were obsolete, since

settlement had reached as much as a hundred miles to the west. A new line of defense was necessary and a new chain of forts was built. Fort Belknap and Fort Phantom Hill were established in 1851; Fort Chadbourne in 1852, and Camp Cooper in 1856. Three of these posts, Fort Belknap, Camp Cooper and Fort Phantom Hill were located on the Brazos River. The latter two were on the Clear Fork of the Brazos, where this story largely occurs. The fourth, Fort Chadbourne, is important to this story primarily because it was the birthplace of John Chadbourne Irwin, who grew up to be a key figure in the history of Fort Griffin. Irwin was born on February 7, 1855, while his father was first sergeant of Company C, Second Dragoons, "and because I was said to be the first child born at the fort, they named me John Chadbourne, after my father and the fort."[1]

In September 1859, former Sergent John Irwin moved his family to Camp Cooper, where he obtained a contract to supply beef to the post. He built a house downriver and settled.[2] Although the post itself was a rundown collection of tents and semi-permanent stone huts, it was important as the center of the recently established reservation for the Southern Comanches.

The inspector general of the Army, Colonel J.K.F. Mansfield visited Camp Cooper shortly after its founding in 1856, when it was garrisoned by two companies each of the Second Cavalry and First Infantry, under the command of Lieutenant Colonel Robert E. Lee. In his report, Mansfield wrote:

---

[1]"The Frontier Life of John Chadbourne Irwin," as told to J.R. Webb, fall and winter, 1934, in J.R. Webb Papers, hereinafter cited as John Chadbourne Irwin to J.R. Webb.

[2]Ibid.

The post is very well commanded by Col. Lee & in good discipline. It labours under the disadvantage of being in an open camp in winter & poor water in summer & dry seasons which cut off the crops of summer vegetables. It is 40 miles from Fort Belknap and is located on the Comanche reservation. As soon as these Indians get settled down in houses, and permanently established, these troops might be better located, say at fort Belknap, where there are accommodations...

The Indians in this region are the Wild Comanches but recently brought by the Agent on this reservation on the Clear Fork of the Brazos. They number 500 souls & at present [are] friendly & promise to remain under [control of] the Agent, Capt. J.R. Baylor, who resides among them.[3]

Unfortunately for the fate of the Comanche reservation, as well as for a second reservation established for the Brazos tribes near Fort Belknap, Baylor was one of Texas' most notorious Indian haters. He was unnecessarily harsh with his charges, and was fired by the superintendent, Robert S. Neighbors, who then assumed personal control. Neighbors was tough and realistic, but was equally compassionate. This compassion earned him the enmity of the growing number of settlers in the Upper Brazos Valley, and the fire was fanned by the vindictive Baylor. Two days after Christmas 1858, a group of whites slipped onto the Brazos reservation and fired into a group of sleeping Indians, killing four men and three women. Baylor announced he intended to destroy the Indians. On May 23, 1859, there was a confrontation in which five whites and one Indian were killed.[4]

---

[3]M.L. Crimmins, "Col. Mansfield's Rept. of the Insp. of the Dept. of Texas in 1856." *Southwestern Historical Quarterly,* Vol. XLII, No. 4, Apr. 1939, pp. 369-373. Lee later commanded the Confederate States Army of Northern Virginia.

[4]Walter Prescott Webb, *The Texas Rangers,* pp. 169-170; James L. Haley, *Texas, An Album of History,* pp. 147-148; Charles M. Robinson III, *Frontier Forts of Texas,* p. 42.

John Chadbourne Irwin in his old age, standing by the old forge from Camp Cooper, which has been shot full of holes by buffalo hunters. 1930s photo from Ben O. Grant, *Early History of Shackelford County.* Courtesy Hardin-Simmons University, Abilene, Texas, and Dean Lawrence Clayton.

As Neighbors struggled to keep the settlers and reservation Indians apart at Belknap, he faced a totally different problem around Camp Cooper. This was raiding by Northern Comanches, Kiowas and other plains tribes who had never accepted the reservation. Failing to understand the implications of annexation, these tribes considered themselves at peace with the United States, and thus free to use U.S. territory as a base for raids against their traditional enemies, the Texans. Pursued by troops or Rangers, they would often hide on the Camp Cooper reservation. To aggravate the situation, the southern bands often left the reserve.

On January 17, 1858, Neighbors described the problem at length in a report to Charles Mix, acting commissioner of Indian Affairs in Washington.

> ...my investigation shows that there have been stolen and driven off from our frontier, since the 1st of November, about 600 head of horses, and that seven persons have been killed or captured by Indians in the same time...The amount of property destroyed and driven off is estimated by our citizens at at [sic] least $60,000, without taking into consideration the lives that have been sacrificed...
>
> Although your department has been notified frequently that the northern bands of Comanches, Kioways, &c., were hostile, and, in addition to their attacks on our frontier settlers, rendering our roads across the State to El Paso unsafe for travellers, as well as the transportation of the mails, they have received their annual presents at Fort Atkinson [Kansas], amongst which was a portion of arms and ammunition, thus arming them the better for their attacks. It is certainly time that this policy should be abandoned, and active military measures adopted to coerce those hostile bands into subjection, and to force them to abandon their predatory habits; and I would again urge this subject upon your immediate attention.
>
> As it appears clear that all the Indian depredations this fall have been committed by Indians who do not properly belong to the State, but intruders from the United States Indian Territories, our citizens are preparing their papers, and claims will be urged against the general government for indemnity for the losses they have sustained.[5]

---

[5]Claims for Spoliations Committed by Indians and Mexicans, House of Reps. Report No. 535, May 18, 1860, p. 5.

Caught in the middle, between whites and hostile tribes, the Indians of the Camp Cooper and Brazos reservations found themselves in a dangerous position. For their own protection, Neighbors closed the reservations, and in the summer of 1859, transported his charges to the Indian Territory. His concern cost him his life. On September 14, shortly after his return, he was assassinated on the streets of Belknap, the town which had grown up around the fort. His murderer, Edward Cornett, was indicted for the crime, and was himself killed by Young County Sheriff Edward Wolffarth while resisting arrest.[6]

The raids along the Brazos continued. On March 6, 1860, Colonel Lee, now acting commandant of the Department of Texas, wrote the chief of staff, General Winfield Scott:

> On the night of the 17th February the mule-yard at Camp Cooper, over which a sentinel was posted, was broken in and the whole herd driven off. Twenty-three of the animals were recovered by a party sent at daylight in pursuit, but the remainder, forty mules and three horses, were not overtaken. The force at the post was so much reduced by scouts then out that the detachment sent under Lieutenant Lowe, adjutant of the regiment, was principally composed of the band.[7]

The following night, Lee noted, all the remaining animals at the former Comanche agency were stolen. Major George H. Thomas, commanding Camp Cooper did not believe they had been stolen by Comanches left on the reservation. Instead, it was pointed out that the horses were found to have been sold at Bent's Fort, on

---

[6]Barbara A. Neal Ledbetter, *Fort Belknap, Frontier Saga*, pp. 87, 91-92; Robinson, p. 42.

[7]Claims for Spoliations..., House Report No. 535, p. 8.

the Arkansas north of Fort Atkinson.[8] This clearly indicated the raids along the Clear Fork had originated outside of Texas.

Despite the problems with Indians and with a growing number of white outlaws as well, the federal government was deactivating the military posts across Texas. Fort Phantom Hill, badly situated to start with, had been closed as early as 1854. In 1859, Fort Belknap was deactivated and left with only a maintenance detachment. Protection of the Upper Brazos area rested with federal units at Camp Cooper, and with state troops, who placed a substantial drain on Texas finances. As Representative John H. Reagan of the House Committee on Indian Affairs reported to Congress, "The State has now in the field a force supposed to amount to near or quite a thousand men, at State expense. The State treasury is exhausted."[9]

But the difficulties did not discourage settlement, and in fact, the frontier line was being pushed farther to the west. Newton Givens, a captain in the Second Dragoons at Camp Cooper, founded the Stone Ranch in 1855, and started the first cattle herd in Shackelford County.[10] Givens had followed the line of defense almost from the beginning, having been given the job of closing down Fort Croghan at Burnet on the original line in 1853, and closing down Fort Phantom Hill the following year. With the establishment of the reservation at Camp Cooper, he saw a market for beef. But the government would not give a contract to a commissioned officer, so he gave up the ranch in 1859.

---

[8]Ibid.

[9]Ibid., p. 2.

[10]Ben O. Grant, "Early History of Shackelford County," M.A. thesis, Hardin-Simmons University, p. 116, hereinafter referred to as "Grant."

Ultimately it came into the possession of Watt Reynolds, whose family would figure prominently in local affairs.[11] Others moving into the area included Joseph Beck Mathews, who brought his family in 1858, Judge J.C. Lynch and James Greer on Hubbard Creek some forty miles to the south, and Judge W.H. Ledbetter, who set up a salt works. There was a regular contact with the outside world by the Butterfield Overland Stage Line, which came through Camp Cooper en route from St. Louis to San Francisco.[12]

Although the future looked hopeful in West Texas, relations between the northern and southern states were deteriorating. Texas left the Union in January 1861, and the following month, United States troops were ordered to turn federal property over to the state. At Camp Cooper, Captain S.D. Carpenter, then commanding, prepared to make a stand. However, orders arrived from departmental headquarters in San Antonio, and Carpenter surrendered the post on February 21. Soldiers were paroled and allowed to march out under arms and with personal effects. The balance of the goods at the post appear to have been looted within the next few days. Command eventually fell to Ranger Captain J.B. (Buck) Berry, a veteran Indian fighter, who remained until April 1862, when the post was abandoned for good.[13]

With the soldiers gone, the frontiersmen of the area settled back into their routines, and life went on as usual. Then a curious thing happened which would profoundly affect the local economy some fifteen years

[11]Frances Mayhugh Holden, *Lambshead Before Interwoven*, pp. 36-41; Robinson, pp. 40,44; John Chadbourne Irwin to J.R. Webb.

[12]John Chadbourne Irwin to J.R. Webb; Don H. Biggers, *Shackelford County Sketches*, p. 5.

[13]Holden, *Lambshead*, pp. 90-92; Biggers, p. 65.

hence. As John Chadbourne Irwin recalled, there had originally been few buffalo in the area.

> But after the soldiers left, they came in by the thousands. I have seen them in their migration both south and north pass for a week at the time, passing all day long by the thousands. The bulls would be in the lead, always coming ahead of the cows, and sometimes on the migration south, the old bulls when they reached here would be weak and would die in the Clear Fork bogs. Have seen them die there so bad that we could not eat the fish from the river...I remember that my father used to make me go out and keep the old buffalo bulls off the calf range around the house.[14]

Commenting on the same phenomenon a few years later, Sixth Cavalryman H.H. McConnell wrote:

> I learned from the old settlers that it was only of late years that buffalo had been numerous in this region, the theory accounting for the vast herds that at this time [1867] and up to, say, 1878, covered all Texas west of the Brazos, was that the building of the Union Pacific road had divided the range and driven millions of them south.[15]

In a way, this was correct. The buffalo were moving away from the areas of heavy settlement, seeking new ranges where they could live undisturbed. With them came the Indians, who took advantage of the absence of troops to raid into the area. The bulk of the Confederate forces were fighting in the east, and the burden of frontier defense fell to small units of Rangers and locally organized "Minutemen."

For awhile, the Indians appeared content with stealing horses or cattle. Some lives were lost, but if the raiders could make off with livestock while avoiding bloodshed, they were generally content. By 1864, however, the situation was serious. Federal scouting

---

[14]John Chadbourne Irwin to J.R. Webb.
[15]H.H. McConnell, *Five Years a Cavalryman*, p. 65.

parties in New Mexico and those sent out by Texas authorities both reported a build-up of weapons and provisions among the Kiowas and Comanches, and an ominous consolidation of camps. Still, the frontier was reasonably quiet in the immediate Brazos area, and most settlers had little reason for concern.

The storm broke on October 13, when the two tribes swept through the heavily populated area along Elm Creek in Young County, above Fort Belknap. It was a murder raid, and before it was over, twelve settlers had been killed and eight carried off into captivity. Some ranch houses underwent sieges lasting several hours before the marauders moved on. The slaughter would have been much greater had not some settlers ridden ahead and given warning, allowing several families to flee to stronger positions or hide in the thickets along the creek.[16]

The Elm Creek Raid was one of the worst in Texas history, and came as a profound shock to the settlers. Watt Reynolds' son, Phin recalled:

> There was a great deal of excitement on the frontier after this, and many people left out for the interior. We had no soldiers to protect us, or rangers, as the Confederacy was short on man power. So, the settlers were called together for a discussion as to ways and means of protection for their families. It was decided to "fort up," that is, come together and build their houses close together for protection against the Indians. Thus, it was that the various forts, as they were called, sprung up along the outer edges of the frontier, and in our section there were Ft. Davis, Owls Head, Clark, Pickettville, Mugginsville, and Hubbard. None of these had any soldiers or artillery. The men, though, were supposed to do scout duty.
> Our family moved to Ft. Davis, which was built on the

---

[16]Ledbetter, *Fort Belknap*, pp. 110-118; John Chadbourne Irwin to J.R. Webb.

banks of the Clear Fork in the northwestern part of
Stephens County...Built in the form of a square, it
consisted mostly of picket houses. At first, they started a
stockade around the houses, but this was never completed,
for the scare somewhat died down.[17]

Settlers from Fort Davis did their share of fighting.
One group clashed with a band of Comanches on the
Double Mountain Fork of the Brazos, killing five, along
with a Mexican and a black who were with the Indians.
George Reynolds took an arrow in the groin, and
carried the arrowhead for fourteen years, until a
surgeon in Kansas City removed it. Another man was
also wounded, but not so seriously. "I saw the party
upon their return to Fort Davis after the fight," John
Chadbourne Irwin said. "They had gruesome evidence
of their victory, as they had the scalps of their victims
and all of the Indian equipment."[18]

But encounters between Indians and whites were
not always so bloody, and at times it almost seemed as
though the Indians had a sense of humor. One time in
1865, they dropped in uninvited on a dance at Fort
Davis.

Not only were they uninvited, but they danced, left, and
took with them the horses of the invited guests. They were
the Comanches, and not until the dance was over and the
men who had come from a distance went for their horses
and found them gone was the boldness of the Indians
discovered, or rather suspicioned. Not until the next morning was the discovery made that the Indians had, only a few
yards under the hill from the fort, enjoyed the fiddlers'
music with a dance of their own as mocassin tracks circling

[17]Phin W. Reynolds to J.R. Webb, May 1936, Apr. 1938, in J.R. Webb Papers,
hereinfter cited as P.W. Reynolds to J.R. Webb. A historical marker by the Visitor's
Center at Fort Griffin State Historical Park tells of these forts. Fort Davis and Fort
Clark are not to be confused with the U.S. Army posts of the same name.
[18]John Chadbourne Irwin to J.R. Webb.

about clearly evidenced. They had made no disturbance to attract anyone's attention.

The war ended in 1865, but little changed on the frontier. U.S. troops who arrived in Texas came as an army of occupation, to subdue and pacify the whites rather than contain the Indians. As a result, the tribes were able to shove the frontier line of defense fully one hundred miles east of where it had been in 1860. Knowing they would receive no protection from the United States government, the settlers continued to huddle inside their makeshift forts and make the best of things. Over the next eighteen months, Kiowas, Comanches, Lipans and Kickapoos cut a swathe of death and destruction the length of the frontier from the Red River to the Rio Grande, while Radical Reconstructionists entrenched themselves in Austin, and federal authorities denied the gravity of the Indian problem.

The Radicals found their champion in Brevet Major General Charles Griffin, who bcame military commandant of Texas on January 24, 1867. He fell into a bitter dispute with Governor J.W. Throckmorton, a Texas Unionist whose own loyalty to the United States was unimpeachable. But Throckmorton chose a middle road in his policies, which angered Griffin and the Radicals. The general began undermining him with General Phil Sheridan, divisional commander. Soon, orders came down that only the military could call an election, and that all appointive offices had to be submitted to the military for approval. Throckmorton was removed from the governorship, and E.M. Pease was appointed to replace him.[20]

---

[19]P.W. Reynolds to J.R. Webb.
[20]Charles William Ramsdell, *Reconstruction in Texas*, pp. 140, 149-161, 174-175.

If the frontier was neglected during this time, it was not totally forgotten. Units of the Sixth Cavalry passed the Christmas holidays of 1866 in Austin, preparatory to marching up to Jacksboro, some eighty miles east of Camp Cooper. During the stay in Austin, Lieutenant Henry H. Wilson from Massachusetts died of unspecified causes, and his body was shipped home for burial.[21] This in itself was a minor incident, but is of some interest in light of subsequent events.

The Sixth rode out of Austin on December 28, arriving in Jacksboro about 3 p.m., January 14, 1867. Trooper McConnell described the "blackened chimney-stacks and ruined ranches" the soldiers passed during those last miles, evidence of the Indians they had been sent to control.[22]

Once on duty, the regiment set about seeing what could be done about military installations. After several false starts and relocations, Fort Richardson was finally established about a mile south of Jacksboro. Attention also turned to Fort Belknap, where the government hoped to reactivate existing facilities. McConnell recalled the stir when U.S. troops arrived after an absence of more than half a decade.

> The few natives living at or near Belknap gazed at our command with astonishment, particularly the children. The grown persons had resided there before the war, and had seen no soldiers since the old garrison marched out in 1861;[23] none of them, I think, had participated in the rebellion, except as "rangers" in frontier service.

The post itself had a sobering effect on the troops.

> The buildings were all of stone, and very substantially

---

[21]McConnell, p. 42.

[22]Ibid., p. 50.

[23]It was actually the maintenance detail; the garrison had left in 1859.

finished, but it having been abandoned at the outbreak of the rebellion and not occupied since except by rangers during the war, at the time I first saw it, it was dilapidated and ruinous. The commissary and forage house were in a tolerable state of preservation, but the quarters and hospital were roofless and most of the wood work had been removed...when [the adjoining town] was occupied by settlers and the fort filled with troops I have no doubt it was, as I was informed it had been, the prettiest frontier post in Texas, but now desolation reigned supreme. Sand, sand everywhere; dead buffalo lying on the parade ground; a few ancient rats and bats looked on us with an evil eye for disturbing their repose, and my first night's rest in the old commissary was broken by visions of old infantry sentinels stalking ghost-like on their beats, and the wind howling through the broken roof.[24]

Still, the post could have been rebuilt, except for one major factor. Fort Belknap was essentially waterless. The Brazos itself was undrinkable, and the well in the fort often ran dry. Finally, General Griffin authorized the garrison to move to a more suitable location. A survey was made of the surrounding area, and a spot was chosen near the Clear Fork of the Brazos, thirty miles upstream from Belknap. Two creeks fed the Clear Fork and the command could draw sufficient water from them.

On the afternoon of July 31, 1867, companies F,I,K and L of the Sixth Cavalry arrived from Fort Belknap and camped on a flat area between a mesa and the river. "This flat was soon found to be unsuited for a company on account of the marshy condition of the ground during the rains," the medical officer reported. "Upon the recommendation of the Medical Officer the command was removed to a neighboring height;

---

[24]Ibid., pp. 66-67.

situationed about a quarter of a mile from the river."

The new post was initially called Camp Wilson, in memory of the lieutenant from Massachusetts. But after Griffin died of yellow fever on September 15, 1867, it received a new name—Fort Griffin.[25]

[25]Post Medical Report, Fort Griffin, Texas, "Locality and History."

2

Outlaws and Indians

Military bases are located primarily for strategic reasons. As they grow older and the particular emergency lessens, they may or may not be developed for the convenience of officers, politicians and surrounding communities. It is almost a natural law that some posts are "plum" assignments while others are viewed as the closest thing to hell without actually being there.

On the Texas frontier, San Antonio was the best place to pull garrison duty. Surrounded by a major city, and one where the Army was appreciated, a soldier's life could be very pleasant. If San Antonio was not possible, Fort Davis, in the Trans-Pecos boasted a healthy climate.

The opposite extreme was Fort Griffin, which had absolutely nothing of any benefit for officer or soldier. Its role was to protect the frontier, pure and simple.

When Fort Griffin was founded, the Quartermaster Department intended it should be built entirely of stone. Steam sawmills were shipped in, along with window sashes, doorframes and tools. A "number of mechanics" were assigned to do the job.[1]

Unfortunately, that's as far as it got. In December

[1]Post Medical Report, Fort Griffin, Texas, "Locality and History."

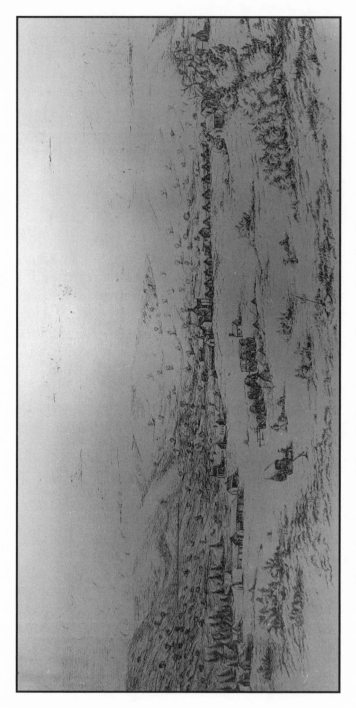

The military post of Fort Griffin. Courtesy Eugene C. Barker Texas History Center, University of Texas, Austin.

1869, the post surgeon was able to cite an 1867 report in describing the place.

> The fort is built entirely of wood and the lumber, from which the buildings were constructed, was sawed in the mill, put up by the fort quartermaster in the neighborhood, and being green at the time it was worked up, the boards have warped and shrunk to such an extent in some instances as to cause many buildings to leak badly.[2]

Nothing was ever done to improve the situation. The slipshod wooden buildings were never replaced, were in constant need of repair, and were a continual source of irritation to officers and men alike, for as long as the fort existed. Only a few key structures, such as the commissary, headquarters, bakery, and magazine were ever built of stone, and these are the only walls of the original post still standing. The men lived in heat in the summer and cold in the winter. The sudden shift from "hot and sultery days" to cold, damp nights in the fall was blamed for at least one attack of dysentery by the very limited science available to medical officers at the time.[3] They did, however, suffer from various ailments which could, in fact, be blamed on the heat, cold or damp, and on lack of proper bathing facilities. Soldiers washed in the surrounding creeks or in the Clear Fork when weather allowed, and remained dirty when it did not.[4]

Supply was another problem in the early years, before the town grew up nearby. In September 1869, the medical officer reported that the post trader was out of stock on many items. While the quality of the food was never a source of serious concern, he did

---

[2]Ibid., Dec. 17, 1869.
[3]Ibid., Sept. 1869.
[4]Ibid., various dates, 1869-1874.

point out that fresh vegetables were "very limited; and are brought generally from the eastren part of the state and consist of a few sweet potatoes and occasionally onions which are sold at extravagant prices." The hospital staff was constantly on alert for signs of scurvy, although it never assumed serious proportions.[5]

Normally, the sick list at Griffin was not long, which is surprising since its entire medical history was a catalogue of filth and squalor. When W.R. Steinmetz arrived to assume the duties of post surgeon in January 1870, he found the hospital in chaos. The store room was so disorganized and heaped with trash that he had to build a new one before he could go in and inspect the property.

"Upon cleaning the store room," he wrote, "two fire buckets were found containing—in a state of decomposition—one specimen of a portion of the entrals of some beef cattle, the other [a] human being which were thrown out and the buckets thoroughly cleansed and disinfected."[6]

Five years later, Surgeon D.C. Caldwell found overall conditions had not changed, except, perhaps, for additional complications caused by women and gunslingers in the town which had grown up down on the bottom by the river.

> The habits of the Men might be materially improved, by the removal of a number of Lewd Women living in the vicinity of the post. The Soldiers not only become demoralized by frequenting these resorts but some of them have already contracted venereal diseases and one soldier was wounded by a pistol ball in one of these drunken haunts. It would, in my opinion be a great benefit to the garrison and

[5]Ibid., Sept. 1869, and various dates.
[6]Ibid., Jan. 1870.

improve the discipline and health of the post if these disreputable women were removed by the Authorities, either Civil or military.

As for the post itself, Caldwell said:

> The general police...has been very much neglected, refuse matter of all kinds has been allowed to accumulate in the ravine and side of the hill west of the Cavalry Corral, and offal of every kind has been scattered around everywhere. In my opinion all this refuse matter ought to be removed to a greater distance from the garrison, and its further accumulation prevented by larger police parties...
>
> I would also recommend that the grounds around the laundresses quarters should be better policed, and their quarters be inspected more frequently by their Company Commanders.[7]

Although post records consistently attest to the character of the laundresses, they were often prostitutes. In fact, the laundry service was accepted as a way to practice prostitution with government sanction. It is no coincidence that the red light districts of military towns—most notably the one at Jacksboro near Fort Richardson—were often known as "Sudsville." It is unlikely the laundresses at Fort Griffin were any different from those of other frontier posts, at least until the town got started and began to offer more variety.

From the official point of view, troops entertained themselves with hunting parties, billiards and band concerts during the early days.[8] But the very existence of a military post meant that it was only a matter of time until squatters and parasites established themselves nearby and cashed in on the Army payroll. The

---

[7]Ibid., March 21, 1875.
[8]Ibid., Nov. 1869, and various dates.

medical report for May 1872, is perhaps the first official reference to the settlement at Fort Griffin, using the name by which it would become famous.

> The Valley through which the Clear Fork comes, is known as the "Bottom" or "Flat" and is the seat of the Tonka-wa Camp & the settlement of "Squatters." Prominent amongst the latter is a saloon keeper named Peppert alias "Joe Bowers" a desaparate or noted desperado who had already murdered two men in cold blood within sight of the waving Stars & Stripes, without any effort being taken by the military authorities to bring him to justice.[9]

"Peppert" was known as Kit Peppard or Joe Bowers, depending on whom he talked to. He claimed to be from Prescott, Arizona. While in Griffin, he had a running feud with a man named J.B. Cockrell. At one point, he went gunning for Cockrell, but succeeded only in shooting his horse out from under him. He was more successful on February 18, 1872, when he shot Cockrell through the right lung. The victim was taken to the post hospital, where he remained until March 2. By May 3, Cockrell was well enough on his feet to make an end to it. He got his Winchester, went into Peppard's saloon and was met with a fatal blast from the latter's shotgun.

During his brief stay in the Flat, Peppard also killed John Carter, a black wood contractor for the post, and a second white man whose name is not recorded. Notwithstanding, he came and went on the government reservation as he pleased, much to the indignation of the medical officer.[10]

The Tonkawas referred to were Indian scouts retained by the Army and headquartered at Fort Griffin.

---

[9]Ibid., May 1872.
[10]Ibid., P.W. Reynolds to J.R. Webb.

In 1854, there had been perhaps six hundred of them living on the Brazos Reservation at Fort Belknap. Like the other tribes, they had been moved to the Indian Territory when the reservation closed. Several years later, a dispute with the plains tribes led to a general massacre, which fewer than a hundred Tonkawas survived. This remnant fled to the white settlements for protection.

From then on, the Tonkawas nursed an undying hatred of the plains Indians. Under the leadership of Chiahook (Charley) and a mixed-blood named Johnson, they gave outstanding service during field expeditions. In Griffin, however, men and women alike roamed the streets of the Flat "in a beastly state of intoxication."[11] Saloons kept them liquored up in violation of federal law, and it was not always safe to go into town unarmed. On one occasion, a party of drunken Tonkawas even fired on an infantry lieutenant.

Back on the post, the soldiers' lives were governed from dawn to dark by the post sundial and by bugles. Reveille was at daybreak, followed by stable duty. Sick call came at 6:45 a.m.; breakfast, 7 a.m.; drill from 7:30 to 8:30, followed by morning-long fatigue for anyone not on guard. Guard was mounted at 9:30 a.m.; water call, 11:15 a.m.; orderly call, 11:45 a.m.; and so on throughout the day. Stable duty was repeated at 4 p.m.; with retreat at sundown; fatigue at 8:15 p.m.; taps at 8:45 p.m.; and guard inspection and mounting at 9 p.m.[12] Stable call was perhaps the most thoroughly detested part of a cavalryman's day, with drill running a close second. Even men who liked riding hated the daily regimen on horseback.

---

[11]Biggers, p. 27; "beastly state of intoxication," Post Medical Report, May 1872.
[12]Medical Report, Nov. 1869.

There was a reason for the constant drilling, since the Indian threat was always close at hand. In 1867, cattleman Charles Goodnight was putting together a herd at the old Camp Cooper agency, when Comanches shot into the camp one night. An arrow hit the neck of a man who was sharing Goodnight's bunk, and the next morning, arrows found under the bunk indicated

Chiahook or "Charley," one of the chiefs of the Tonkawas at Fort Griffin. Courtesy Texas State Archives.

they had been shooting low, to get the men as they slept.[13]

On March 1, 1868, Comanches swept deep into Stephens County, and killed a man named George Hazelwood on Sandy Creek, south of present-day Breckenridge. Hazelwood put up a fight before they got him. About forty spent cartridge cases from his rifle were found around his body. Continuing on west, they killed Phil Reynolds (no relation to the Shackelford County Reynolds family), an employee of Judge W.H. Ledbetter's salt works, twenty-five miles from Fort Griffin. Reynolds was out in his wagon gathering wood when they killed him.

The Ledbetter salt works itself was attacked on March 2. The Indians were hidden behind the banks of the nearby creek about sunrise, when employee Nep Thornton came out toward them. Some distance from the house, he spotted an Indian's head as the latter peered up over the bank. Trapped in the open, Thornton drew his pistol, took careful aim and fired. The Indians began shooting. Thornton knew he had no chance if he turned and ran, so he squatted down to steady himself and carefully fired whenever he had a target. Judge Ledbetter came to the door of his house and maintained a continual fire, while his wife reloaded his guns. Whenever the Indians tried to surround Thornton, a blast from the judge sent them behind the banks again. Thus Thornton was able to slowly withdraw to the house.

Eventually, the Indians decided the salt works was not worth the effort or possible losses, and broke off the fight. Phin Reynolds claimed the judge loaded the kingbolt of his wagon into an old cannon he had on the

---

[13]P.W. Reynolds to J.R. Webb.

place, and fired it after them in a parting shot. His daughter, Martha Judy Ledbetter Shelton, had no recollection of that. She did remember that he caught a bullet across his stomach.[14] Apparently it did not seriously injure him.

Once the Indians had left the vicinity, Thornton and Sam Lindsey walked to Griffin and notified the troops. Captain A.R. Chaffee took five officers and sixty-two troopers of the Sixth Cavalry in pursuit, accompanied by Ledbetter and the Tonkawas. The hostiles were trailed to a point about eight miles south of present-day Haskell, where the soldiers attacked at dawn, March 6. The Comanches were routed. The Tonkawas went into a frenzy and could not be brought under control until they had literally butchered every Comanche they could lay their hands on. Among the dead was a black man, wearing the scalp headdress of a chief. He was lying on a travois and showed a recent gunshot wound. Since a man on a travois had been seen during the attack on the salt works, Ledbetter speculated he had been shot by Hazelwood.

The black man was identified as Cato, who lived at Fort Concho, but who would frequently and mysteriously disappear. Apparently he was raiding with the Indians whenever he was gone. It was also learned that he was the husband of Indian Kate Gambel, a prostitute who later worked in the Flat at Fort Griffin.[15]

The raids slackened as the decade came to a close, but the frontier still simmered. As 1871 dawned, attacks became "unusually frequent, and were marked by a

[14]Biggers, p. 53; P.W. Reynolds to J.R. Webb; Martha Judy Ledbetter Shelton to Joan Farmer, in notes to Biggers, pp. 101-102.

[15]P.W. Reynolds to J.R. Webb; Martha Judy Ledbetter Shelton to Joan Farmer, in notes to Biggers, pp. 101-102.

degree of ferocity unknown during recent years."[16]
Citizens of Texas protested to such an extent that the
chief of staff, General W.T. Sherman decided to visit
the area himself. Accompanied by General Randolph
Marcy, who was familiar with the frontier, Sherman
arrived in Texas in April, and made a wide sweep of the
posts along the line of defense. Marcy kept a journal,
which was largely routine as far as Fort Griffin, where
the party arrived on May 14. There, he noted the
deplorable state of quarters, as others would before
and after his visit.[17] Yet during the same period, two
scouting parties, one of state troops and the other of
Fourth Cavalry, were out from Fort Griffin in search
of hostiles, and so missed the commanding general's
visit altogether.[18]

Marcy himself formed an accurate idea of the
problem as the party proceeded toward Fort Richardson. In the seventy miles between the two posts, he
noted "the remains of several ranches . . . the occupants
of which have been either killed or driven off to the
more dense settlements by the Indians. Indeed this
rich and beautiful section does not contain today so
many white people as it did when I visited it eighteen
years ago, and if the Indian marauders are not punished, the whole country seems to be in a fair way of
becoming totally depopulated."[19]

Sherman's party crossed the Salt Creek Prairie east
of Fort Belknap, and arrived at Fort Richardson
without incident. The following day, however, a wagon

---

[16]McConnell, p. 273.

[17]C.C. Rister, "Documents Relating to General W.T. Sherman['s] Southern
Plains Indian Policy, 1871-1875," in *Panhandle-Plains Historical Review*, Vol. IX, 1936,
p. 18.

[18]Medical Report, May 1871

[19]Rister, *Panhandle-Plains Historical Review*, IX, pp. 18-19.

train taking a load of corn to Fort Griffin was attacked on the same road, and seven teamsters were massacred. A wounded survivor stumbled into Fort Richardson and gave Sherman a detailed account. Investigation showed the raiders were reservation Indians from Fort Sill. Three of the responsible chiefs were arrested. One was killed in an escape attempt. The other two were extradited to Texas, tried and sent to the state penitentiary.

The massacre convinced Sherman that the Army's job must shift from containment of the Indians to suppression. He found the instrument of his new policy in Colonel Ranald Mackenzie, the brilliant young commander at Fort Richardson. Mackenzie respected the Indians as fighters, but was not awed by them. He understood horses as well as they, and was a master of hit-and-run tactics. Although nominally post commander at Richardson and regimental colonel of the Fourth Cavalry, he was in fact the military viceroy of West Texas. His cavalrymen were scattered from Fort Brown near the mouth of the Rio Grande, to Fort Concho in the west, and up through Fort Griffin and Richardson. He utilized them and commandeered what he needed as he saw fit. His high-handedness and his honesty earned him the hatred of many ranking officers and bureaucrats. But he had the backing of the public and support in the War Department. For the first time, the Indians were on the defensive.

Mackenzie made several field expeditions, using Fort Griffin as his central base for thrusts into the unknown reaches of the plains. To facilitate his supply, he established what became known as the Mackenzie Trail, which crossed the Clear Fork at a point near Griffin called Mackenzie Crossing. Although his initial forays failed to subdue the plains tribes, they provided valuable information for the final showdown which would eventually come. Meanwhile, raiding continued.

On May 9, 1872, Hank Smith, hay contractor for the Army at Fort Griffin, headed his wagons out toward a stand of post oaks near the Abel Lee place in Stephens County, where he intended to get wood for hay frames. The Clear Fork was up, and he couldn't get his wagons across, so he postponed the project. This inconvenience saved his life.[20]

At the Lee place, Abel Lee was sitting on his front porch reading. A young man was visiting one of his daughters, while Mrs. Lee and the other children were "enjoying a social hour." A group of Kiowas slipped up behind a bank and opened fire, killing Lee where he sat. Mrs. Lee came to the door and received a mortal

---

[20]H.C. Smith to Lillian Ernest, November 28, 1872, in H.C. Smith Papers, Panhandle-Plains Historical Society.

Hank Smith. Courtesy Panhandle Plains Historical Society, Canyon, Texas.

arrow wound. Fourteen-year-old Rebecca Lee was killed, and Susanna, 16, Millie, 9, and John, 6, were captured. The boyfriend managed to escape.[21]

Word reached Fort Griffin and troops were turned out. Smith guided them across the flooded Clear Fork, and he and John Chadbourne Irwin accompanied them to Lee's. Both parents had been scalped, and one of Mrs. Lee's arms had been severed. Irwin helped bury the bodies, then served as part of the delegation which helped secure the return of the surviving children about a year later.[22] Two months after the Lee massacre, Smith fought off an attack on his hay camp on Bush Knob Creek in Throckmorton County.[23]

The military established a camp in the ruins of old Fort Phantom Hill as a subpost of Fort Griffin, and scouting expeditions stepped up. More and more troops from Griffin were detailed to serve with Mackenzie.[24] Under this pressure, the Brazos Valley became quiet, and in 1873, Mackenzie was sent to Fort Clark to police the Rio Grande area. Back on the Clear Fork, soldiers amused themselves as best they could. The post trader operated a saloon for those who wanted to stay on the reservation and avoid going into town. Jacob Howarth, an Englishman who served as sergeant in the 11th Infantry under the name of Howard, recalled that soldiers went down to the Flat "only at our own risk, and the citizens had to be on their behavior if they came to the Fort. They governed on the Flat and the military on the Fort."[25]

[21]Odie Mintara, "A Life Near the Heart of Texas History: J.C. Irwin Recalls First Hand Many Memorable Events of Pioneer Days," in J.R. Webb papers; William H. Leckie, *The Military Conquest of the Southern Plains*, pp. 152-163.

[22]Mintara, "J.C. Irwin," Leckie, p. 162.

[23]H.C. Smith to Lillian Ernest.

[24]Medical Report, June 8, 1871, and various dates, 1872.

[25]"Old Soldier Writes of Fort Griffin Experiences," in *The Albany News*, May 30, 1935.

It was a brief respite. On February 25, 1874, a scouting party led by Lieutenant Colonel George P. Buell, post commander at Fort Griffin, engaged and defeated a party of hostiles along the Double Mountain Fork of the Brazos. Eleven Indians were killed and fifty-six head of stock were captured.[26] Meanwhile, up on the high plains, in Kansas and the Indian Territory, the situation was a powder keg.

Much of the problem was due to a sudden upsurge of buffalo hunting. It had been sporadic until 1870, with most of the kill going for meat or robes. But that year, J. Wright Mooar and John Wesley Mooar, brothers from Vermont, managed to establish a regular market for hides as well. Orders poured in from the east, and the great slaughter of the northern herd began. Dodge City boomed as the center of the hide trade. For the plains tribes it was a disaster, because their entire economy was built around the buffalo. Still, they did

[26]Medical Report, Feb. 11, 1874.

J. Wright Mooar. Courtesy Scurry County Museum, Snyder, Texas.

nothing, since the southern herd below the Arkansas River was virtually intact.

But the Mooar brothers had elevated the hide trade to a major industry, and the slaughter reached assembly line proportions. Within three years the northern herd was almost wiped out and hunters began venturing south of the Arkansas. They had even gone so far as to establish a supply and shipping center at Adobe Walls in the Texas Panhandle, which was easing the trade away from Dodge City.

Those most directly affected were the Kiowas and Comanches. But the Arapaho and southern Cheyennes were having problems as well. White outlaws, notably a group led by Hurricane Bill Martin, were making off with their livestock. The Indians took legal action, but could get no satisfaction from government authorities.[27] Added to that was a general discontent caused by government pressure to cease raiding. This deprived the young warriors of their means of gaining prestige in the tribes. Faced with the end of their preferred way of life, the normally pragmatic and secular Comanches began listening to a prophet named Isa-tai. He was said to speak directly with God, to be capable of miraculous powers, such as levitation and the ability to vomit an unlimited supply of bullets. He told the tribes God could make them victorious over the whites, and they themselves would be bullet-proof.

After a few preliminary attacks, Isa-tai convened a council of Comanches and Cheyennes. Whiskey flowed, speeches were made and pipes were passed, and when it was over, the two tribes decided to settle scores with the Tonkawas at Fort Griffin. Word reached James

[27]James L. Haley, *The Buffalo War*, pp. 21-22, 45.

Haworth, agent for the Kiowas and Comanches, who alerted the command at Griffin. The Tonkawas were moved into the fort up on Government Hill, and the hostiles adopted an alternative plan—an attack on Adobe Walls.

The assault began at dawn, June 27, 1874. After a day of fighting, the Indians gave up and withdrew, leaving thirteen of their own people dead. Obviously, Isa-tai's promises of invulnerability were worthless against the superb marksmanship of the buffalo hunters, and his prestige was gone. But the tribes wanted revenge.[28] The Red River War had begun. Soon after, the Kiowa war faction threw in with the hostiles, while in Washington, orders went out for mobilization.

The government's campaign was five-pronged, with forces moving in from Kansas, the Indian Territory, New Mexico and Texas to catch the hostiles in the middle. Mackenzie stormed up from the south and out onto the plains, and Fort Griffin became the nerve center of his column. Throughout the summer and fall, troops passed through, and wagons rumbled back into the fort for more supplies. By January 1875, when Mackenzie's worn-out Fourth stumbled into Fort Richardson, the campaign was virtually finished.

Although sporadic raids continued throughout the 1870s, they were minor compared to what had gone before. The Red River War signalled the end of Indian military might on the Southern Plains. The leading war chiefs were exiled to Fort Marion, Florida.

Fort Griffin's heyday as a military post was drawing to a close. The era of the Flat had begun.

---

[28]Leckie, pp. 190-194.

3

The Buffalo Hunters

The close of the Red River War opened the entire Texas plains to the buffalo hunters. The leaders of the uprising had been deported to Florida. The tribes themselves were confined to the Indian Territory, and Fort Elliott was established in the Texas Panhandle to make sure they stayed there. The hunters could now operate on a much wider front, sweeping across the plains like a scythe. This threw the most convenient marketing center from Dodge City to Fort Worth. And the point offering most convenient access to the hunting grounds to the west and Fort Worth in the east was Fort Griffin. Thus the center of the Texas hide trade moved from Adobe Walls to Fort Griffin, and the legend of the Flat was really born.[1]

On Christmas 1874, even as the Army was still mopping up from the Red River campaigns, twenty-year-old Joe McCombs led the first hunting expedition out of Fort Griffin. Despite his youth, McCombs was already an experienced frontiersman, having come to the Flat two years earlier. He got some idea of the vast extent of the Southern buffalo in the fall of 1872,

---

[1]Frederick W. Rathjen, *The Texas Panhandle Frontier*, pp. 167-168.

while working on a railroad survey west of Belknap. The party encountered a herd which members estimated at 50,000 head, and at one point got caught up in a stampede.

Now, two years later, McCombs was hunting hides, with John Jacobs and John William Poe as skinners. "From the low ground, I would creep, hunting afoot and getting into scattered bunches of from ten to 100 head," McCombs recalled. "I would always shoot the leader of the herd, usually a bull, and if I could get him, the bunch or herd would start milling until another assumed leadership and headed out and then I would try to get him, the idea always being to keep shooting while they were milling, but to get a leader in order to keep the milling going on."[2]

Most of the buffalo had gone farther south at that time of the year, but in two months, McCombs had managed to kill 700. They returned with the hides to Griffin, then headed farther west, beyond Fort Phantom Hill. This time, they stayed out until May 1, and got 1,300 hides. At the end of the season, they sold 2,000 hides at Griffin, for $2 for each robe hide, and $1.50 apiece for the others. "They were the first hides of any consequence marketed at Fort Griffin," he noted.[3]

It didn't take long for others to catch on, and in 1875, the Mooar outfit was ready to hunt from Fort Griffin. Before leaving the post, the commanding officer, Colonel George P. Buell told Wright Mooar to stay within 20 miles, since the military still feared Indian trouble. In fact, Wright later recalled that Buell

---

[2]"Frontier Life of Uncle Joe S. McCombs," Earl Vandale Collection, Barker Texas History Center.
[3]Ibid.

threatened him with arrest if he strayed beyond. "My brother was behind and when he caught us, he asked what Buell had said. I told him, but that he would never come after us. We all had those Sharps Big 50's and could have made quite a stand."[4]

As we saw in Chapter 2, the Mooars had perfected the buffalo hide trade, and in some ways were directly responsible for the Red River War. Their operation made Joe McComb's pioneering effort of a few months earlier seem nothing more than a camping trip. The outfit had sixteen wagons, and Wright Mooar hired nine outlaws to work it. "I worked outlaws a good deal," he explained. "You never saw a lazy one. When one is down and out and tells you he wants to work, he will work, attend to his business, and make a good hand as long as he is with you. I got some of them in Griffin and some out in the brush, and then I pulled out 140 miles from the Fort."[5] So much for Buell's orders.

Mooar may have trusted outlaws, but others didn't. Writing of them in 1874, Cordelia Adair, whose husband John became Charles Goodnight's partner in the JA Ranch, commented, "Many of these men are the roughs of the frontier, criminals flying from justice, notorious ruffians and murderers, and the settlers are more afraid of them than of the Indians."[6]

Henry Herron, who also hunted, had mixed feelings. "Most of the buffalo hunters were all right, regardless of what has been written about them. However, there were some tough ones amongst the skinners on the

[4]J. Wright Mooar to J. Evetts Haley, Nov. 25, 1927, hereafter referred to as "Mooar, 1927."

[5]Ibid.

[6]Cornelia Adair, *My Diary, Bath, England*, cited by J. Frank Dobie in *A Vaquero of the Brush Country*, p. 136.

range. A lot of them were refugees from justice and out there to avoid arrest. Fort Griffin was the closest town to the buffalo range, and there was little law out there. During '78 and '79, Shackelford County had attached to it, for judicial purposes, 13 counties to the west, but did not have an officer on the buffalo range. One bad character that drifted into our camp whom I was later to assist in trailing down and arresting in Coleman County, was one Dee McDonald, a member of the McDonald Brothers gang that committed a brutal murder at old Fort Belknap."[7]

By and large though, most men on the range were professional hunters and skinners, and went about their business with a ruthless efficiency that would do any assembly line proud. The hides poured into Fort Griffin and the buffalo hunters had money to spend in the stores and dives of the Flat. The period of 1876-1879, when the hunt was in full swing, was probably the most prosperous time in the brief history of Fort Griffin.[8]

The men who cashed in most were the suppliers, and the greatest of these was Frank E. Conrad. A native of Rockford, Illinois, Conrad had been taken to Tampa, Florida, as a child. Upon the death of his parents, he was brought to San Antonio to live with an aunt and uncle, and learned the merchant's trade as a clerk in his uncle's store. Shortly after the war broke out, he joined Hood's Texas Brigade and served until the end.

Conrad was about 24 years old when he was

[7]J.R. Webb, "Henry Herron: Pioneer and Peace Officer During Fort Griffin Days," Webb Papers, hereafter referred to as "Henry Herron."

[8]"The Frontier Life of John Chadbourne Irwin" as told to J.R. Webb; "Henry Herron," both in Webb Papers.

Frank E. Conrad. Courtesy Old Jail Art Center and Archive, Albany, Texas.

appointed post trader at the newly reactivated Fort McKavett, just north of what is now I-10 near Sonora. Two years later, he moved to Fort Griffin to assume the same position there, and so was able to get in on the ground floor when the buffalo boom started. Meanwhile, Charley Rath had expanded his interests from Kansas to Fort Griffin, and teamed up with Conrad to form Conrad and Rath.

The company had a warehouse and magazine attached to the store, where it kept 30 tons of lead and five tons of powder. One hunting party which came through the store in 1876 included a tall, lanky fugitive from family problems named Pat Garrett. Garrett, who would later gain fame as the man who killed Billy the Kid, was hunter for a party which also included Skelton Glenn, Luther Duke and Joe Briscoe. He bought a Winchester from Conrad for $50, while the others paid $56 apiece for Sharps. They also bought ammunition and provisions, all of which the firm supplied.[9]

Conrad and Rath not only outfitted the hunters, they bought and shipped the hides, thus making money both ways. But while they were the biggest, they were not the only outfitters in the Flat. Rival F.B. York and Co. offered "Highest Cash Prices Paid for Hides and Furs."[10] Others were William McKamey, T.E. Jackson and E. Frankel. On the opposite end, in Fort Worth, the firm of Gurley and Co. served as commission and hide merchants, receiving as many as 1,000 hides a day. The Fort Worth *Democrat* carried daily quotes on hides from the Galveston exchange.[11]

For recreation, the Flat offered gamblers, saloons and soiled doves to help the hunter forget the hard months on the plains, and to relieve him of his well-earned cash. "I've seen men and women dancing there in the dance halls without a bit of clothing on," hunter J.W. Woody recalled.[12]

Henry Herron observed, "The buffalo hunters and their skinners, the drovers, and the cowboys going up the trail had plenty of money to spend, and they spent it recklessly. For instance, a year or so after I arrived in Fort Griffin, I saw a buffalo hunter come to town one day and market his season's kill for $1,500, and the next morning he had to borrow money for his breakfast. The gamblers had gotten all of it. The ordinary fellow did not have the ghost of a show in those gambling halls. Most all of the games were crooked, and if they could not get it one way, the would another.

[9]"Frank E. Conrad," Webb Papers; Rye, p. 220; Leon C. Metz, *Pat Garrett, The Story of a Western Lawman*, pp. 8-9, 12-15.

[10]Fort Griffin *Echo*, Jan. 4, 1879.

[11]Rye, p. 220; Fort Worth *Democrat*, Apr. 13, 1878.

[12]J.W. Woody to J. Evetts Haley.

Frequently, they would get their victims drunk and 'roll' them and take it away from them in that way. The back of every saloon was a gambling hall, and there were so many saloons that the number I have given at this time [eight or ten] is just my recollection. The number varied from time to time."[13]

But the hunters themselves were not innocents. In one case, in February 1876, Young County Sheriff Richard Kirk came to Fort Griffin to get a local tough called Buffalo Bill.[14] As J.W. Woody remembered, "They were both crack shots. They met there at Fort Griffin and Bill knew he had come to arrest him. Both had Winchesters. They were about ten feet apart and had their guns held pointing at each other from their hips. The sheriff said, 'Bill, lay your gun down or I'll have to shoot.' Bill pulled the trigger and hit the sheriff in the heart, while his shot hit Bill in the middle of the forehead."[15]

Even the range was not safe. In addition to Indians and outlaws, hunters had to content with each other. It was a hard, often frustrating life. They got on each other's nerves, and sometimes someone would crack. Pat Garrett learned this the hard way, in November 1876. The hunting had been poor for awhile and cold, damp weather had set in. Garrett was chafing on his legs, and was depressed and moody. Joe Briscoe had gone down to wash his clothes in an arroyo and had come back with fingers frozen and mumbling to no one in particular about being unable to get anything clean in the muddy water. Garrett answered with a

[13]J.R. Webb, "Henry Herron."
[14]"Bill" was common both as a name and an alias in the 19th Century West. This particular Buffalo Bill was no relation to William F. (Buffalo Bill) Cody.
[15]J.W. Woody to J. Evetts Haley.

remark about Irish intelligence—or lack of it. Briscoe, a solid Irish Catholic, started swinging and was promptly knocked into the mud by the six-foot five-inch Garrett. Briscoe got on his feet and again was sent sailing into the mud. After the scene had been played several times, Garrett tried to extricate himself. By now, though, Briscoe was in a complete rage and went after him with an ax. Running as hard as he could, Garrett managed to grab his rifle, then turned and fired into his pursuer. The impact sent Briscoe spinning into the campfire, mortally wounded.

The frightened Garrett grabbed a horse and took off into the plains. He returned the next day, and after consulting with his companions, decided to ride into Griffin and turn himself in. Within a few days, he was back, saying the authorities had declined to prosecute.[16] Whether Garrett actually turned himself in is a matter of conjecture. Given his record, he probably did. And given their record, the officials in Griffin simply wrote it off as just another killing on the plains.

The basis of this world of violence, money and hardship was the hunt, which continued unabated and with brutal precision. When the railroad reached Fort Worth on July 4, 1876, shipping became all the easier. And as the 1876 season got underway, the industry really boomed.[17] The Jacksboro *Frontier Echo*, which covered the news from Fort Griffin, predicted, "Big business in hides for fall and winter" in 1876.[18] On November 8 of that year, the Fort Worth *Democrat* carried this notice:

---

[16]Metz, *Pat Garrett*, pp. 16-17.

[17]Wayne Gard, "How They Killed the Buffalo," in *American Heritage*, Aug. 1956, p. 38.

[18]Jacksboro *Frontier Echo*, July 21, 1876.

FROM THE WEST

Freighters Wanted.

The Buffalo Hunt the
Largest Ever Known

The Hides Coming to
Fort Worth.

FORT GRIFFIN, Freighters are wanted to transport buffalo
hides to Fort Worth. The hunt is the largest ever known.
Countless thousands of buffalo cover the prairies. Ten
thousand hides are now on their way to the railroad, and
thousands await transportation to Fort Worth.[19]

Some 1,500 hunters were out on the plains that
season. Joe McCombs remembered "buffalo hunters
were coming in pretty thick. The northern hunters
were following the herds on their migration south . . .
All the time now, the herds were being drifted west by
the hunters who were hard after them from morning
till night. We could hear the guns of other buffalo
hunters occasionally, but most of them were to the
east of us. I always tried to keep on the outer edge."[20]

By early spring, hides were stacked on some four
acres around the Flat. "All the space not occupied by
houses was covered with racks of buffalo hides, representing the winter's hunt, ready to be transported to
Dallas, Denison or Fort Worth, 150 to 200 miles
distant," Edgar Rye said.[21]

A variety of rifles was used to bring in this tally of
hides. When the industry first began out of Dodge
City, the best rifle was the .50-caliber Springfield,

[19]Fort Worth *Democrat*, Nov. 8, 1876.
[20]Gard, "How They Killed the Buffalo," p. 38; "Uncle Joe McCombs," Vandale
Collection.
[21]Rye, p. 28.

designed as an infantry weapon. This was replaced in 1873 by the .45-70. But according to Wright Mooar, "They were too light...and I wrote to Sharp that we wanted a heavier bore. He said a larger one would not be true, but he made this heavier gun."[22] Thus was born the .50-caliber Sharps or Big Fifty, which became *the* buffalo gun, and almost wiped the animal from the face of the planet.

Most hunters loaded their own shells, increasing the range by upping the charge. The factory load was 90 grains of powder, but hunters reloaded them as high as 110 grains. Used with a telescopic sight, the effect was devastating. In addition, the Mooars loaded theirs by wrapping the bullets in paper instead of greasing them, to prevent a lead build-up inside the barrel. "The bullets were made with a concave butt. When the barrels of our guns got so hot they began swelling, the bullets with this concave butt would be expanded when shot by the charge of powder, thus filling the barrel and making it true."[23]

Every hunter agreed that it was necessary to kill the leader of the herd. While Joe McCombs and most others contended it was generally a bull, J.W. Woody said it was "always a cow. If you could shoot that cow with what we called a 'lung shot,' she would trot around for a little while and then die. When you got the leader in this way, you had what was called a 'stand,' and the other buffalo wouldn't leave until they

---

[22]Mooar, 1927. Mooar's claim is disputed in Robert Foster's introduction to "Buffalo Guns in Texas, the Sharps Rifle Company Texas Letters, 1875-1882," in *The Museum Journal* XII, 1970, p. 8. However, Foster offers no reason for his dispute. On the contrary, there is ample reason to believe Mooar. Manufacturers often tailor a product according to the advice of an expert in the field, and Mooar was the acknowledged leader of the hide industry.

[23]Mooar, 1927; Wayne Gard, *The Great Buffalo Hunt*, p. 107.

had to. If you didn't kill the leader first they might travel on you."[24]

Wright Mooar did not specify a gender on the leader, although he always used the word "he." "The leader was not always in the lead of the bunch. Sometimes he would be behind. There was something about him that told me he was the one. Sometimes there would be two or three leaders to a bunch, and sometimes I failed to pick the leader, but as soon as I shot I could tell whether I had picked the right one or not. If I had not, I quickly threw another cartridge into my gun and killed the leader as soon as I could, so as to get a stand. As soon as I killed him, the others would stop running."[25] Then the slaughter began.

A Sharps rifle weighed 10 to 14 pounds, depending on caliber. The hunter rested it on his knee, or more often on a rest stick. He also carried as many as 100 rounds in a double width belt for the day's hunt. When the hunter went on to another stand, the skinners moved in.

"Using their six-shooters the skinners killed the wounded. A few motherless calves that had escaped the bullets were knocked in the head." Each skinner carried two knives and a sharpening steel and were "artists in their line. With one stroke of the knife they encircled the hock above the hoof, then a quick movement of the hand split the hide down each leg and along the animal's belly to its underjaw. Then, with a large, curved skinning knife, the hide was removed in the incredibly short time of from five to eight minutes." In some cases, nothing was saved except the tongues

[24]"Uncle Joe McCombs," Vandale Collection; J.W. Woody to J. Evetts Haley.
[25]J. Wright Mooar to J. Evetts Haley, Feb. 11, 1925, hereafter referred to as "Mooar to Haley."

Buffalo skinners at work on the Texas plains, 1874. Courtesy George Robertson, Texas State Archive, Austin.

and hides. "Consequently, from $15 to $20 worth of fine meat was destroyed to save a dollar hide. After the work of removing the hides was finished each man carefully wiped his knife and returned it to the scabbard attached to his belt. Then began the operation of salting and rolling the hides, preparatory to hauling them to camp."[26]

Some camps were organized to the point of having a specialist called a ripper, who would slit the skin and then move on to the next carcass while the skinners finished the job. According to J.W. Woody, "There were men in the country who could skin 100 buffalo a day, and do their own ripping. The Anderson and Long outfit, which had a camp at Big Spring, had a man who could skin 100 any day."[27]

Not everyone wasted meat. Some parties were meat hunters, who would go out in the fall and take the animals for their meat. "There was a lot of buffalo meat freighted out of this country," Woody said. S.P. Merry told of making a vat by propping up a hide with four sticks, then packing it with as much as 1,500 pounds of boned meat. This was salted, with a little saltpeter added for color, then covered with another hide. After curing for ten or twelve days, it was smoked, with a smokehouse also made of hides.[28]

Freighters with bull teams took the hides to Fort Griffin, where other freighters hauled them on to Fort Worth. "You hardly ever saw a team under 18 or 20 yoke of steers and five or six trail wagons," Woody said. "They used from that on up to 40 yoke of steers and about 10 trail wagons. They freighted both hides

[26]Henry Herron to J.R. Webb, Webb Papers; Rye, pp. 260, 264-265.
[27]J.W. Woody to J. Evetts Haley.
[28]Ibid.; S.P. Merry to J. Evetts Haley.

and meat. One man drove all those cattle, but they usually had a cook and a herder. The driver rode a pony up and down the line of steers. If he wanted them to go to the left, he hollered 'Woho-o-o-o-a.' If he wanted them to go to the right, he hollered 'Hike.'

"Men came out to the range and bought hides right at your camp. We sold nearly all our hides right here on the range."[29]

In October 1877, word filtered along the range that a white buffalo had been seen near the Mooar camp on the headwaters of the Clear Fork. Frank Conrad offered $100 for the hide. Wright Mooar got it on October 7. It was a four-year-old cow which he found in a herd of 4,000. The hide was turned over to a tanner in Dodge City.[30]

The peak year was 1877. Joe McCombs struck out in September, with skinners, stakers, 1,000 pounds of lead and five kegs of powder. His take that season was 9,700 hides, which he had to sit on, since the price was falling. He finally sold them for a dollar a hide, which was lucky, considering the price in Galveston was depressed.[31]

"That was the last year of the big kill and the biggest year for the buffalo hunters in Texas," McCombs said. "The hunters followed the herds north that summer and back again in the fall. All the time they were being hunted."[32]

Already, the massive slaughter was worrying many people. As early as 1875, a conservation bill to protect the buffalo was introduced in the Texas Legislature.

---

[29]J.W. Woody to J. Evetts Haley.
[30]Mooar to Haley; Rye, pp. 221-222.
[31]"Uncle Joe McCombs," Vandale Collection; Fort Worth *Democrat*, 1877-1878.
[32]"Uncle Joe McCombs," Vandale Collection.

To the military, such a bill was unthinkable, since it protected the economy of the warring plains tribes. Lt. Gen. Phil Sheridan rushed to Austin to oppose the bill.

Speaking of the hunters, Sheridan told lawmakers, "These men have done in the last two years, and will do in the next year, more to settle the vexed Indian question than the entire regular Army has done in the last thirty years. They are destroying the Indians' commissary; and it is a well known fact that an army losing its base of supplies is placed at a great disadvantage. Send them powder and lead, if you will; but, for the sake of lasting peace, let them kill, skin and sell until the buffaloes are exterminated. Then your prairies can be covered with speckled cattle and the festive cowboy, who follows the hunter as a second forerunner of an advanced civilization."[33]

The bill was defeated and the hunters continued to kill, skin and sell. Soon, as Sheridan predicted, the plains around Fort Griffin were "covered with speckled cattle and the festive cowboy."

---

[33]Gard, *The Great Buffalo Hunt*, pp. 214-215.

4

The Toughest Town
in the West

Up until 1874, the Flat was a typical military scabtown, a motley collection of saloons and brothels which fed off the soldiers. There was no real commercial center in the sense of the town it would later become, and it existed primarily as an irritant to Army medical officers. The entire area was under the jurisdiction of the post commander at Fort Griffin, and the military kept things reasonably quiet within the immediate vicinity of Government Hill. But with the organization of Shackelford County, things started to get really interesting.

On paper at least, Shackelford County had existed since 1858. However, it was attached to various other counties for judicial purposes, the latest being Jack County on May 1, 1874.[1] The problem was that Jacksboro was some seventy miles away, and administration from there was impractical. Consequently, local citizens met under a tree in what is now the recreational area of Fort Griffin State Park and petitioned Jack County Court for separation. The petition was

[1]Grant, pp. 1-2.

Fort Griffin, late 1870s, showing both the military post and the Flat. The large compound in the right foreground is Frank Conrad's emporium. Edgar Rye woodcut, courtesy Old Jail Art Center and Archive, Albany, Texas.

granted, and on September 11, 1874, the people of Shackelford County elected officers. Shortly thereafter, Fort Griffin was designated county seat pro-tem until an election could fix it permanently.[2]

With an organized county, the area outside the post boundaries passed from military rule to civilian and the Flat really got moving.

Western towns were made tough by any of four basic industries and the money they brought; these were the military, buffalo hunters, mines and cattle. Fort Griffin had three of the four, with mines being the only thing lacking. Once the Flat was firmly established in the military trade, the buffalo hunters moved in, and finally, the cowboys came. All had cash and were ready to spend it. Residents of the Flat were more than willing to help them do it, and if this meant fights, vice and an occasional killing, that was part of the risk of doing business. As Jimmy M. Skaggs noted in his thesis, "The Great Western Cattle Trail to Dodge City, Kansas," "Should the nights grow peaceful, the town stood in economic peril."[3]

Although one could spend hours reading through the old docket books of the District Court in Albany, an examination of Shackelford County's first two days of court sessions will show enough of the situation as it was in Fort Griffin. Among the indictments returned on June 8, 1875, opening day, were:

> The State of Texas vs. Long Kate and Minnie—Fighting in a public place, to wit: a grocery.
> The State of Texas vs. Frank Smith, Griffin, Long Kate, Mollie McCabe and Minnie—Keeping a disorderly house, to

[2]Ibid., pp. 105-106.
[3]Jimmy M. Skaggs, *The Great Western Cattle Trail to Dodge City, Kansas*, p. 86.

wit: a house where vagabonds & prostitutes resort for the purpose of public prostitution.

The State of Texas vs. Thom Grise and Maggie Thriss— Living together in Adultery.[4]

And on day two:

The State of Texas vs. Wm. Reed, Wm. Henderson and Maggie Marshall—Keeping a disorderly house, to wit: a house where vagabonds and prostitutes commonly resort for the purpose of public prostitution.

The State of Texas vs. Thos. Grise & [Isaac] Blum— Permitting diverse persons to play at a game with cards with each other in a house under their control & when used by them for retailing spiritous liquors.[5]

The State of Texas vs. Owen Donly, Lynch, Curley & Hurricane Bill—Playing at a game with cards in a house used for retailing spiritous liquors.

The State of Texas vs. Jim Oglesby, Hurricane Bill, Ellen, Etta, Long Kate, Minnie Liz and Mollie McCabe—Keeping a house of Public Prostitution the same being a disorderly house.[6]

In nearly every case, the defendants received the proverbial slap on the wrist. Indeed, it almost seemed as though the court, through its fines, was actually licensing these activities. Prostitutes were hauled in on the average of once a year on accumulated indictments, fined $100 per indictment and set free for another year. Mollie McCabe was once arrested on four counts of keeping a disorderly house, found guilty and fined $100 on each count. These fines replenished the coffers of Shackelford County and guaranteed the girls would be left alone.[7]

[4]Shackelford County, Minutes of the District Court, Vol. A, 6-7-[18]75 to 3-1-[18]84, p. 3.

[5]Ibid.

[6]Ibid., p. 4.

[7]Grant, p. 84-85; Jacksboro Frontier Echo, Aug. 11, 1876.

A prominent figure in the Fort Griffin underworld was Hurricane Bill Martin. He had come from the Midwestern Plains where he had been the ringleader of a gang of horse thieves, gun runners and bootleggers. He was one of the more notorious outlaws whose continuing raids on Southern Cheyenne livestock had been a factor in throwing that tribe into the hostile camp during the Red River War.[8] Edgar Rye called him "as slick a rascal as ever escaped justice...He played the winning hand in a game with cards, whether he had the trumps or was compelled to run a bluff with his six-shooter and scoop in the stakes without showing his hand."[9]

Hurricane Bill could sometimes push too far, though. One morning he went into the Bee Hive Saloon, where he ran into his sworn enemy, Mike O'Brien. Both were already drunk and Mike was cursing the black porter. Feeling particularly brave, Bill made some slanderous remarks about Irishmen and blacks. Apparently Mike went for his gun and so did Bill, when it suddenly dawned on them that neither was armed. Bill dashed for his picket shanty across the street, while Mike ran into the back room of the Bee Hive for his buffalo gun. He got one shot off, just as Bill rounded the corner.

Mike went out into the middle of the street, sat down in the dust and began shooting Bill's shanty to pieces with the heavy buffalo gun. Inside, Bill crouched under a window and attempted to return fire with his Winchester. The fight attracted a substantial audience. One spectator, another drunken Irishman named Bill Campbell, took a bottle and a glass out to Mike "to stiddy yez nerve." Mike stopped shooting long enough

---

[8]James L. Haley, *The Buffalo War*, pp. 45-46.
[9]Edgar Rye, *The Quirt and Spur*, p. 74.

for a drink, then went back to blasting away at Hurricane Bill's shanty. Finally, he ran out of ammunition and went back into the saloon in disgust, leaving Hurricane Bill to ponder his demolished shanty and an approaching hangover and, no doubt, to face the wrath of his wife, Hurricane Minnie.[10]

Hurricane Minnie was a prostitute. Bill appears to have served as her husband, paramour and pimp. Meanwhile, she openly consorted with gunslinger John Selman. Bill had no great enthusiasm about marrying her, and apparently did so primarily at the behest of his sometime employers, the Shackelford County Vigilance Committee. For this, he resented the committee thoroughly.[11]

The Bee Hive Saloon was Hurricane Bill's favorite haunt. According to Henry Herron, it was the principal saloon and dance hall of the eight or ten that operated in the Flat at any given time.[12] A sign painted on the front said:

> Within this hive we are all alive,
> Good whiskey makes us funny,
> If you are dry step in and try
> the essence of our honey.[13]

"Lewd women infested these places, and all of them had their little huts or shanties, which sprawled along the bank of the Clear Fork of the Brazos River," Herron recalled.[14]

Indeed, as late as 1880, census reports showed Shackelford County with a male population of 1,199

[10]Ibid., pp. 75-76.

[11]Leon Metz, John Selman, p. 79.

[12]J.R. Webb, "Henry Herron, Pioneer Peace Officer from Fort Griffin Days," typescript in Webb Papers, herefter referred to as "Henry Herron."

[13]P.W. Reynolds to J.R. Webb.

[14]Webb, "Henry Herron."

and a female population of 838.[15] Therefore it is hardly surprising that so many of the early court records, newspaper accounts and recollections of pioneers center around prostitutes. They went by a variety of names—frail sisters, fallen angels, soiled doves. And like Minnie, most of them consorted with outlaws in various ways over and above their usual professional services. "Kate Gambel was one of the notorious women of this type, and as she was part Indian, she was better known as 'Indian Kate,'" Herron recalled. "I was to learn that she stood in with some of the officers of the law for protection. And I was to learn that her house was a rendezvous for cutthroats and murderers and all other lawless characters. She would double-cross the officers as well as the criminals when it suited her purposes, but quite naturally, she would favor the criminals."[16]

The prostitute's life was a hard one, perhaps one of the hardest on the frontier. The prime age was fifteen to thirty, after which they were generally considered too old.[17] Alcoholism, drug addiction and suicide were often their lot.[18] They were women of no past and few prospects.

There were other, more mundane hazards as well. On November 19, 1875, the Jacksboro *Frontier Echo* reported:

> Last Friday morning about 4 o'clock a fire broke out in Mollie McCabe's "palaces of beautiful sin." She owned the building, which was entirely consumed, together with most of her household goods and wardrobe. Cause, carelessness of one of the damsels of spotted virtue.[19]

---

[15]Fort Griffin *Echo*, Feb. 5, 1881.

[16]Webb, "Henry Herron."

[17]Anne M. Butler, *Daughters of Joy, Sisters of Misery*, p. 15.

[18]Ibid., p. 67.   [19]Jacksboro *Frontier Echo*, Nov. 19, 1875.

Like other women, prostitutes were often the center of quarrels between men and perhaps did their share to provoke them. In 1876, the *Frontier Echo* reported that two black soldiers from the post came to blows over a "damsel of color." The fistfight led to gunplay, and one of the soldiers was killed.[20]

The diverse racial and ethnic groups thrown together in the Flat were themselves a source of tension and violence. Griffin's population was largely Southern, and the war was only recently over. Incidents occurred there which were repeated all over the South for the next hundred years. Typical was the death of William Corn, a black man who was killed by the sheriff "as he was attempting to evade arrest."[21] Indians were another target. A Lipan living with the Tonkawas by the fort was reportedly murdered by "an Irish woman and a Mexican."[22]

Sometimes the poor and downtrodden found champions and avengers where they might be least expected. One such case arose when a man named Houlph came to town, tied his horse to a hitching rack and got drunk. Houlph partied throughout the day and all night. The next morning, the horse was still tied to the hitching rack, suffering from thirst. A Tonkawa unhitched him and started to lead him around the side of the saloon to water, when Houlph came to the door and demanded to know what the Indian was doing. Before there was any reply, Houlph snarled, "I'll tend to my own damn horse," and killed the Tonkawa. No one much cared what happened to an Indian, so Houlph was simply thrown in jail until he sobered up.

[20]Ibid., March 10, 1876.
[21]Ibid., Oct. 16, 1875.
[22]Ibid., July 7, 1875.

One man did care, and that was John Selman. The Indian was a friend of his. A few weeks later, Houlph was found dead on the prairie. People generally accepted the explanation that his gun had accidentally discharged and killed him. But there were those who said Selman had avenged his friend.[23]

The social problems were particularly acute with the military always present. Soldiers can be a pretty tough crowd, and it was aggravated by the fact that Fort Griffin was a base for black troops. Buffalo Soldiers were generally known for better discipline than their white counterparts, but when they felt slighted, things could get rough. At Griffin, they had plenty of opportunities to feel slighted.

Disaster was narrowly averted on one occasion by a Ranger exercising authority where the military command had broken down. The trouble started when white troops were given passes into town while the blacks were confined to post. Seeing this, the blacks determined they would go as well. When the guard ordered them to stop and threatened to shoot, they went back to their barracks for their weapons. The guard had no choice but to let them pass.

As the Buffalo Soldiers headed into town, Ranger Captain G.W. Arrington appeared with seventy white cavalry, and told the senior Army officer, a lieutenant, to order the blacks back to barracks. He did and they refused. Both sides were armed, and a confrontation appeared imminent. Finally, Arrington himself ordered them back. Soldiers often worked with the Rangers, and these troops may have been accustomed to receiving his orders. At any rate, they gave in and went grumbling back to the fort.[24]

[23]Grant, pp. 83-84.   [24]Ibid., pp. 59-60.

The military sometimes showed an annoying tendency to meddle in civilian affairs. On November 8, 1874, Shackelford County held an election to determine whether the county seat would remain permanently in Fort Griffin, which was near the northern edge of the county, or be moved to a more central location. The central location won, and a site was selected where Albany now stands. Griffinites were not finished however, and obtained a new election in order to regain the county seat.[25]

The election was set for December 31, 1875. But on Decembr 18, at least two protests were sent, one to Senator S.B. Maxey, and the other to Brigadier General Edwin O.C. Ord, commander of the Department of Texas, concerning military interference. Signed by a "Citizens Committee" comprised of C.K. Stribling, Peter Hart, J.N. Browning and Patrick Carroll, both said essentially the same thing. The one to Ord stated:

> An election to fix the county seat of Shackelford County is about to take place. Lieut. Col. Buell, commanding the post of Fort Griffin, is using his official infuence to intimidate the voters by threats. Do you sanction it?[26]

Ord replied:

> If you have charges to prefer against Lt. Col. Buell for using his Official Position to intimidate voters, send them to me and they will be investigated or you can bring case before Civil Courts under Section two thousand and three 2003—revised Statutes, United States.[27]

There is no indication the committee ever followed through. The election was duly held and Fort Griffin failed to obtain the necessary two-thirds vote. The

[25]Ibid., p. 106.
[26]Citizens Committee to Ord, Dec. 18, 1875, in H.C. Smith Papers.
[27]Ord to Carroll, Browning and Hart, Dec. 20, 1875, ibid.

county seat remained in the new settlement of Albany.[28]

With or without color conflicts and official meddling, the Army brought its share of problems to the Flat. Soldiers have historically resented officers and civilians, and an otherwise good soldier might create problems when fortified by liquor. One such case occurred on April 29, 1879.

Company A, 22nd Infantry, had arrived at Fort Griffin that morning, and by early evening, Private Charles McCaffray of Burlington, Vermont, was thoroughly drunk. A lieutenant turned him over to the sergeant of the guard, with instructions to confine him to the guardhouse. But McCaffray escaped from the sergeant and made his way into town. First he went to the house of "an estimable married lady," whose husband was not at home, and offered "a gross insult." Then he wandered down to Conrad and Rath's store, where he insulted Captain S.H. Lincoln of the 10th Infantry. Lincoln's company was scheduled to leave for Michigan the following day, and apparently he didn't want any complications. He chose to overlook the insult. Finally McCaffray asked where to find the garrison.

"Come with me and I will show it to you," Lincoln said, as he took McCaffray by the arm and marched him out of the store. As they reached the front door, McCaffray muttered, "You will be sorry for this, sir."

They made it as far as the sidewalk in front of Conrad and Rath's warehouse, where McCaffray hit Lincoln on the chin, knocking him out into the street. Lincoln pulled his pistol and fired, hitting McCaffray in the left side of the neck. He was taken to the post hospital, where he lived for twenty-two hours, until 6 p.m. the following day.

---

[28]Grant, p. 106.

Lincoln was arrested by civil authorities, posted a $2,000 bond, and left for Michigan on schedule. But a coroner's inquest charged that he "did willfully and feloneously kill and murder said Charles McCaffray without any lawful provocation." A warrant was issued charging him with murder. Ranger Captain G. W. Arrington and Frank Conrad caught up with Lincoln's column, served the warrant and took him to Albany for trial.

The trial took most of the week of May 19. One of the jurors became ill and was excused. Those who remained on the panel determined the killing was justified and recommended acquittal. G.W. Robson, editor of the Fort Griffin *Echo* wrote that the verdict "meets the hearty approval of the large majority of the citizens of the county."[29]

As we will see, Robson was a solid Griffin booster for as long as he lived in the Flat, and his editorials tried to downplay its tough reputation. In one issue, he wrote:

> This town has heretofore had an unjust epithet of a "hard place." During all the trial and hard times in which this place has had to pass through its citizens have always been law abiding people. It was not the citizens of Fort Griffin that brought this name upon us but it was the transient class of men and women who came to and sojourned in the town. To prove this assertion the people of the town have, from the commencement of their trouble, during the whole time and are now paying out of their private purses a salary from $50 to $100 per month for an officer to patrol the town day and night, to keep down riots, fighting, murdering, robbing and other crimes. The trouble is now over and a more quiet and peacable town is not to be found in Texas.[30]

---

[29]Fort Griffin *Echo*, May 3-4, 1879.
[30]Ibid., Apr. 19, 1879.

This was largely wishful thinking on Robson's part. For the Flat's population was largely the "transient class of men and women" whom he blamed for the trouble. Less than six weeks after that editorial, Rangers confronted August Erps on the streets of Griffin. Erps, who was wanted for horse stealing in Medina County, pulled on them and was gunned down. Robson's headline referred to it simply as "Another Killing."[31]

Some of the area's crime had an almost 20th century ring to it. On the night of February 24, 1879, O'Sullivan, post blacksmith at Fort Griffin, returned from market to find his house on fire. The house was on the south end of officers row, and the fire appeared to have been intentionally set to take advantage of a south wind and torch the whole row. The soldiers were busy with O'Sullivan's house when shots rang out and someone shouted, "Commissary on fire." The building was safe, but the sentry on duty said he had found someone trying to start a fire. He got off three shots when the suspect disobeyed a command to halt, but had missed and the suspect got away. During that same period, range fires were reported in the area, which also appeared to be the work of arsonists.[32] There was no particular feud or range war underway at the time, so the reasons behind the fires remain a mystery.

Not every incident led to bloodshed or destruction. Texas honor has always been a touchy proposition, and a good fight could involve some reasonably respectable people. Jim Draper was not necessarily respectable, but he did serve at times as a peace officer, and Robert

31Ibid., May 31, 1879.
32Ibid., March 1, 1879.

A. Jeffress was an attorney who often handled matters for the county. They were hauled into district court on charges of affray. Draper demanded a jury trial and was fined one dollar upon return of a guilty verdict. Jeffress waived a jury, was found guilty and fined $5.[33]

Knives flashed in one incident involving drunken Tonkawas, but no one was hurt. As the *Echo* reported it: it:

> Wednesday last a number of Tonkawa Indians were in town and a few of them obtained whisky [sic]. Grant and Cooper became involved in a quarrel when, Indian fashion, Grant drew his knife on Cooper. Several passes were made but nobody hurt when Constable [John William] Poe put in an appearance and Mr. Indian "lit out like a quarter horse and the longer he ran the faster he got," so Poe says. They returned soon however, and John gobbled onto Cooper and boosed ["calaboosed," i.e. jailed] him. Soon he found old Charley and served him the same way. After keeping them all night and sobering them up, they were turned loose with a kick and a cuff and admonished to "rack out, dad burn you," for camp and sin no more.[34]

There was no way around the fact that Griffin was a tough town. And as long as it was to remain economically viable, it would remain tough. The types of people who enabled it to survive were those who by their very nature contributed to the general lawlessness.

---

[33]Ibid., Apr. 26, 1879.
[34]Ibid., May 31, 1879.

5

Legends of the Flat:
Lottie Deno and
Doc Holliday

Of all the women who haunted the floating world of the Flat, none created more of a stir than Lottie Deno. Years later, she stood alone in the recollections of the old timers.

No one knew Lottie's real name or where she came from, but some thought she was born in Warsaw, Kentucky, on April 21, 1844. This would have made her about thirty-one years old when she arrived in Fort Griffin in 1875 or 1876.[1]

Likewise, opinions differ on her appearance. She was "probably the best looking woman" Mrs. A.A. Clarke ever saw. Lawman John C. Jacobs called her "a wonderful woman. She was on the portly side, a fine looker, and in manners a typical Southern Lady, but didn't always live up to her appearance." On the other hand, Henry Herron, who was deputy sheriff while

---

[1]Nail Papers; John C. Jacobs to J. Marvin Hunter, cited in Biggers, p. 96. A notation in the Nail Papers and Jacobs' statement set the arrival of Lottie as late summer, 1876. John Jacobs recalls being sheriff at the time of her arrival. Actually, he became sheriff in 1880. More than likely, Lottie arrived in late summer, 1875, or early in 1876, when Henry Jacobs was Sheriff.

Lottie was in Griffin, said she was "good looking, but I would hardly call her pretty."[2]

It was her sense of style and decorum which took people aback. Griffinites were used to seeing shady ladies drunk on the streets, fighting and swearing, but Lottie "went about neatly dressed and conducted herself like a lady on the streets," Herron said, adding "I never heard of her taking a drink." Jacobs commented, "She had nothing to do with the common prostitutes that infested such as the Flat under the hill from Ft. Griffin."[3]

Still, Lottie was a prostitute. Herron called her "wicked."[4] Like the lesser denizens of the floating world, she was hauled up and fined $100 for "maintaining a disorderly house." And in February 1878, she paid Judge Clarke $65 for legal representation. One can easily guess the legal problems she must have had.[5]

Lottie arrived in the Flat one evening on the Jacksboro stage, sitting up on the box beside Dick Wheeler, the driver. From then until the time she left, she kept pretty much to herself. In a place like Griffin, which breeds closet romantics, this gave rise to all kinds of rumors. Some said she sent money to her invalid mother in New England, and to help put her sister through a fashionable boarding school. Others claimed she was from an old Southern family and had turned

---

[2]Miss Ollie Clarke to Robert Nail, Nail Papers; Biggers, pp. 95-96; J.R. Webb, "Henry Herron," Webb Papers.

[3]J.R. Webb, "Henry Herron"; Biggers, p. 96.

[4]Robert Nail to Ed Kilman, quoting Henry Herron, "Lottie—and he called her by her first name—was 'wicked.' (His daughter and granddaughter were present; otherwise I believe he would have said *whore* instead of *wicked*.)", Nail Papers. Emphasis is Nail's.

[5]Grant, p. 85; A.A. Clarke's Ledger, p. 165.

to gambling to recoup the fortune lost in the late war.[6] She might even have been a wayward wife.

Whatever her background, she was apparently immune to the scrapes, brawls and killings that went on around her. While Herron maintained she "frequented the gambling halls but not the saloons,"[7] the bulk of the evidence says otherwise. She set up shop in Shannessy's Saloon, and eventually became his mistress.[8] According to Rye, she also played in Wilson and Matthews' Saloon, where she was in a $50-limit game one night when trouble broke out at a nearby table.

The table was being used for a high stakes game, and the pot had reached $500. Everyone had dropped out except Monte Bill and Smoky Joe, a couple of sharps. Monte suggested raising the limit, and Smoky bet his last dollar. With that, Monte laid down three aces and a pair of queens.

Smoky went for his gun, shouting, "Bunkoed by a sneaking coyote from the Badlands, who rings in a cold deck and marked cards when he plays with a gentleman!" Then, invoking a law of gambling, he yelled to the porter, "Take that pot, John!"

"No, you can't play that game of bluff on me!" Monte Bill snarled as he went for his own gun.

The two men blazed away at each other while Lottie dove for the corner of the room. When the smoke had cleared, both Monte Bill and Smoky Joe lay in pools of blood. About that time, the sheriff arrived. Lottie stood up, rearranged herself and went over to meet him.

"Why didn't you vamoose when they pulled their barkers, Lottie?" he asked.

---

[6]Rye, p. 71.; Carl Coke Rister, *Fort Griffin on the Texas Frontier*, p. 136.

[7]J.R. Webb, "Henry Herron."

[8]Nail to Kilman; Rister, p. 136.

"Oh, it was too late, Sheriff. And I was safe out of range in the corner."

"Well, you have your nerve, all right, Old Girl. I don't believe I would have cared to take my chances in that scrimmage."

"Perhaps not, Sheriff, but you are not a desperate woman."

The sheriff agreed, but told her to get home. She left and made her way to her shanty on the outskirts of the Flat.[9]

Lottie wasn't always this lucky. A few years before, about 1872, she had been hit in the face with a cuspidor during a saloon brawl. She was permanently blinded in one eye, giving rise to the frontier expression, "Out like Lottie's eye."[10]

By and large, Lottie managed to stay clear of trouble during her time in Griffin. She had her discreet arrangement with Shannessy, and such "disorderly" business as may have been conducted was handled quietly. Sheriff Jacobs depended on her for information on outlaws hiding in the Flat, which she no doubt accumulated by listening to the talk around her while quietly playing poker. Jacobs trusted her, saying, "She could be relied on to tell the truth."[11]

Then came Johnny Golden.

Johnny was about twenty-two at the time. Like Lottie, his past was a mystery. Herron understood he was from Illinois, while Rye said letters found later on his body showed him to be the black sheep of a rich Boston family. There was also some speculation that he and Lottie might have known each other prior to their arrival in Griffin. Jacobs thought so. He called Golden

---

[9]Rye, pp. 71-73.

[10]Frank X. Tolbert, "Tolbert's Texas" in Dallas *News*, June 10, 1956.

[11]Biggers, p. 96.

"a go-between for outlaws and crooks, and was not in Lottie Deno's class, but Lottie had known him else- where, and [that] he held some kind of club over her was quite apparent to me, and [when] I questioned her about him she brushed me off with the remark that Golden knew her husband's troubles and she had to keep him pacified."[12]

Jacobs is perhaps the only person who has hinted that blackmail was involved. But then he may have been Lottie's only real friend and confidant. To others in the Flat, it simply appeared that Johnny had some money and spent it freely. Whatever the reason, it didn't take long for Lottie to divest herself of Shan- nessy and take up with him. This was more than Shannessy was willing to tolerate.

The saloon keeper made arrangements of his own with Deputy Sheriff Jim Draper and Town Marshal Bill Gilson. Johnny was to be removed for $250.

Draper and Gilson confronted Golden one night in Shannessy's, claiming they had a warrant on him for horse stealing. Johnny retorted that he had never owned a horse. The two lawmen were unimpressed and took him away. Instead of conducting him to the city jail, about twenty yards from the saloon, they claimed they were taking him to the military guard- house at the fort. Johnny never made it. His body was found in back of Hank Smith's wagon yard, about two blocks from Shannessy's.

The stories of the two lawmen varied. They reported a mob had confronted them and had killed Golden, but no one in the Flat believed it. They also said Golden had tried to make a break for it and they had shot him. No one believed that, either. Johnny's friends checked the

---

[12]Henry Herron, "Some Experiences of Frontier Life as Told to J.R. Webb," (hereinafter referred to as "Herron to Webb"), Webb Papers; Rye, p. 73; Biggers, p. 96.

body at the scene, and found the bullet had gone straight through him and into the ground beneath. He had been knocked down and shot.[13] The following day, Gilson and Draper were exonerated in a justice of the peace hearing.[14]

When Lottie heard of the killing, she came apart and blamed herself for it. She gave Jacobs $65 to pay for the funeral, which included a coffin and a new suit. But she stayed in her room as the funeral procession passed. Eight people attended the service. Among the mourners was Bill Gilson.

After that, she became reclusive, rarely going out at all, and having her groceries and other necessary items delivered to her shanty. About a month later, in May 1878, she boarded the stage to Jacksboro and left Fort Griffin for good. Her rent had been paid in advance, so no one felt like opening her room until the sheriff, by now Bill Cruger, came from Albany. Cruger got the key and went in to find a well-furnished bedroom. Pinned to the bedclothes was a note that said, "Sell this outfit and give the money to some one in need of assistance." At least that was Rye's version of it. Herron heard the story, but said he personally knew nothing of the note. Instead, he said the furniture more than likely belonged to Shannessy.[15]

A few months later, Shannessy himself was gone, having sold his saloon to Charley Meyers and taken off to Palo Pinto. There, he planned to "open a first class saloon."[16]

Johnny Golden's father reportedly came to Texas to

[13]Herron to Webb; Nail to Kilman.
[14]Biggers, p. 96.
[15]Rye, p. 75; Herron to Webb; Biggers, p. 96.
[16]Fort Griffin *Echo*, Jan. 4, 1879.

get the true facts surrounding the case. He had gotten as far as Fort Worth when he was warned to leave well enough alone or he would meet the same fate. He did not press the issue.

As for Lottie, Herron said he had heard several accounts that she eventually married and raised a family. However, he personally did not believe them. After Griffin, she hung around Jacksboro for awhile, then vanished from the scene as suddenly as she had appeared, leaving nothing behind but her legend.[17]

If Lottie Deno is a shadowy figure, Dr. John Holliday is thoroughly documented. We know where he was born and where he died and most of what he did during the thirty-five years in between. But Doc Holliday was the type who inspired legend, and when we get to Fort Griffin, we have a hard time separating the legend from reality.

Doc predated Lottie by a year or so, arriving in the Flat about January 1875. At the time, he was twenty-three years old, and in continual pain from tuberculosis. He eased his suffering through alcohol and spent most of his waking hours stewed to the gills.[18]

Holliday had been in a shooting scrape in Dallas on New Year's Day, when he and a saloon keeper named Austin had blasted away at each other from point-blank range. Since both were relatively indifferent shots, no one was hurt. But it seemed to Doc that a trip farther west might be very beneficial to his health.[19] Griffin seemed far enough away from Dallas. The hunters were bringing in tons of hides, and had lots of

[17]Herron to Webb; Rister, p. 138.
[18]Pat Jahns, *The Frontier World of Doc Holliday*, p. 51.
[19]Ibid., p. 49.

money to spend in games with professional gamblers who had nothing to lose. Gamblers like Doc Holliday.

For awhile, Doc prospered. If anyone knew about his shooting scrape in Dallas (and most people probably did), no one seemed to care. There was some slack between vigilance committees, and Sheriff Henry Jacobs plodded along, minding his own business as long as things didn't get too far out of hand. The Flat was in full throttle, and a drunken gambler with a tubercular cough was the least of the sheriff's problems.

Even so, there were times when Jacobs had to make a stab at wiping out victimless crime. Unfortunately, Doc was around when he did. So we find this notation on the docket of the District Court in Albany:

> June 12th 1875
> The Grand Jury, having a quorum present and headed by their foreman, came into open Court (the Court having met pursuant to adjournment, officers present and presiding as before.) And presented the following Bills of Indictment; to wit:
> The State of Texas
> No. 34   vs
> Mike Lynch & Dock Holladay
> Playing together and & with each other at a game with cards in a house in which spiritous liquors were sold.[20]

With that entry, the record on Doc Holliday at Fort Griffin is silent for almost a year. Then, on the docket for May 17, 1876, we find this entry:

> The State of Texas
> No. 34   vs
> Mike Lynch & Dock Holiday
> Ordered by the Court that alias capias issue for defendants Mike Lynch & Doc Holiday.
> Continued[21]

---

[20]Shackelford County, Minutes of the District Court, Vol. A, 6-7-[18]75 to 3-1-[18]84, p. 16.

In other words, Mike and Doc had skipped town.

This is the last *documented* evidence, in fact the *only* documented evidence that Doc Holliday ever set foot in Fort Griffin. But there are gaps. There is supposed to have been a case file on Doc, and it is said to have been detailed. However, it has disappeared from the District Clerk's Office in Albany, and its wherebouts are unknown.[22] Then there are legends passed down among the old families of Shackelford County, and legends die hard. Too many stories have been written about Doc at Fort Griffin. One major film has given it more than passing attention. And finally, much of it seems to be attributed to articles by and interviews with no less than Wyatt Earp, himself.

The essential Doc Holliday legends are two, and they are generally interrelated. One is that Wyatt Earp first met Doc in Fort Griffin, when he needed Holliday's help in rounding up Dave Rudabaugh. Wyatt appears to have related the story to Stuart N. Lake for his biography *Wyatt Earp, Frontier Marshal*. In this case, Wyatt was reminiscing shortly before his death in 1929, some fifty years after the event he described. The Lake version was picked up and embellished by John Myers Myers in his book, *Doc Holliday*. Between these accounts of Lake and Myers, the story has filtered down through book after book, including Carl Coke Rister's *Fort Griffin on the Texas Frontier* and my own *Frontier Forts of Texas*.[23] Then there is the story of how Big Nose Kate saved Doc from a Fort Griffin lynch mob by setting fire to a building. This is told by Lake and Myers as well as by locals in Albany.[24]

[21]Ibid., p. 49.

[22]Bobbie Cox, district clerk of Shackelford County, to Charles M. Robinson III, July 8, 1988.

[23]Stuart N. Lake, *Wyatt Earp, Frontier Marshal*, pp. 191-199; John Myers Myers, *Doc Holliday*, pp. 63-64; Rister, p. 194; Robinson, p. 67.

[24]Lake, p. 198; Myers, p. 71; interview with Joan Farmer, Albany, July 10, 1986.

It is supposed to have happened in late 1877, fully two years after Doc's legal problems were first noted on the district court docket. Wyatt was a lawman in Dodge City, and had come to Griffin on the trail of Dave Rudabaugh, who was wanted by the Santa Fe Railroad for a series of robberies. Since he knew Shannessy, he stopped by the saloon to see if he had any information. Shannessy told him Rudabaugh had already left town, but said Doc Holliday might know something.

"Doc's in my debt for some favors and will help you if I say so," Shannessy is supposed to have said.[25]

Wyatt indicated he was concerned about Holliday's reputation as a gunslinger, but agreed to talk to him. Shannessy sent for him, and Doc agreed to help. Within a week, he told Wyatt that Rudabaugh had gone to Fort Davis in West Texas. Wyatt following him there, only to learn that he had turned back east to Fort Clark. From there, the trail led to Fort Concho, Fort McKavett and once again to Fort Griffin. Wyatt arrived back in the Flat on January 20, 1878, to find that Rudabaugh had doubled back to Kansas, and that Doc and Kate had left for Dodge City in a hurry.[26]

After Wyatt headed west, Doc had run afoul of Ed Bailey, a local tough and popular resident of the Flat from its earliest days. They got into a poker game, in which Bailey would sneak a look at the discards. Under the rules of frontier etiquette, Doc gave notice the cheating had been observed. When his opponent persisted, Doc claimed the pot and Bailey pulled a gun. In a flash, Doc swept up with a knife and slit him open, killing him.

[25]Lake, p. 192.
[26]Ibid., pp. 192-198.

Knowing he was right, and convinced that justice would be done, Doc allowed himself to be arrested. But Bailey's friends were gathering to form a mob, and the local vigilance committee was making plans as well. The marshal didn't dare take Doc to Albany, since he was certain they would be waylaid and the prisoner strung up. So he confined Holliday to his hotel room.

Meanwhile, Kate had managed to secure a gun and a pair of horses. Then she set fire to a barn. The hay and dry wood were engulfed by flames which threatened the entire town, thus drawing the would-be executioners away for firefighting duties. During the confusion, Kate got the drop on Doc's guards, sprang him loose and together they hid by the creek until morning, when they recovered the horses and took off.[27]

These are the recollections of an old man, who was concerned about how posterity would remember him. Another version of Wyatt's story was much less elaborate, and perhaps more factual. In an interview published more than thirty years earlier in the San Francisco *Examiner* on August 2, 1896, Wyatt said:

> It happened in 1877, when I was City Marshal of Dodge City, Kansas. I had followed the trail of some cattle thieves across the border into Texas, and during a short stay in Fort Griffin, I first met Doc Holliday and the woman who was known variously as Big Nose Kate, Kate Fisher, and, on occasions of ceremony, Mrs. Doc Holliday. Holliday asked me a good many questions about Dodge City and seemed inclined to go there, but before he had made up his mind about it, my business called me over to Fort Clark. It was while I was on my way back to Fort Griffin that my new friend and his Kate found it necessary to pull their stakes hurriedly.

Wyatt then discussed the killing of Ed Bailey and

[27]Myers, pp. 61-71.

Kate's fire. However, he admitted the story "was related to me afterward."[28]

The ultimate Holliday-at-Fort-Griffin story is told in the Hal Wallis-John Sturges film *Gunfight at the O.K. Corral* (Paramount, 1957). With a screenplay by Leon Uris, based on an article by George Scullin, the meeting of Wyatt Earp and Doc Holliday in Fort Griffin is completely rewritten. However, Kate's fire is left pretty well intact.

As the movie opens the main titles are superimposed and accompanied by Frankie Laine's vocal. We see three horsemen silhouetted almost in miniature against the vast sweep of the plains. They slowly grow larger and cover more territory, so that when the titles end, they are riding past a cemetery, which a weathered sign identifies as *Boot Hill, Fort Griffin, Texas*.[29]

The horsemen are Ed Bailey (Lee Van Cleef) and two henchmen, who cross a bridge into a sleepy adobe village which is supposed to represent the Flat. Bailey storms into Shannessy's Saloon, where the latter insists they check their guns. At this point, Bailey announces his intention to kill Doc Holliday (Kirk Douglas). But Kate (Jo Van Fleet) has seen them ride in, and heads to Doc's hotel room to warn him.

The scene switches back to the edge of town, where Marshal Wyatt Earp (Burt Lancaster) is riding in from Dodge City. This time, he is looking for Ike Clanton and Johnny Ringo. Upon learning the sheriff has let them ride through unmolested, Wyatt heads toward Shannessy's, where Ed Bailey is pulling on a bottle. By

---

[28]Alford E. Turner, *The Earps Talk*, pp. 2-4. Wyatt Earp's *Examiner* interview is reprinted verbatim in this collection of interviews and depositions by himself and his brothers, James and Virgil. In his notes (p. 18), Turner thoroughly examines the Ed Bailey killing and Kate's fire, and says that while the story may be based on fact, there is no evidence of it having occurred in Shackelford County.

[29]Rye, p. 105, calls it "Bootleg Hill."

now, Bailey is a bundle of nerves and boiling over with hatred for Doc. Shannessy tells Wyatt that Bailey's brother had come in drunk, cheated at cards and pulled a gun on Doc. Holliday promptly killed him, and now brother Ed had come to even the score. Shannessy also mentions Doc had played cards with Clanton and Ringo, and may have some idea of their plans.

Wyatt visits Holliday, who is totally uncooperative. Even so, Wyatt warns him that Bailey has a hidden derringer, then returns to the saloon. Doc follows, and when Bailey pulls the derringer, Doc sends a knife flying into his chest.

Doc is arrested and confined to his hotel room. A mob forms, and Kate asks Wyatt to help. He knocks out the deputy guarding Doc's room, then signals to Kate, who sets fire to a hay shed. The mob is distracted, and they all escape on the road to destiny at the O.K. Corral.

These, then, are the Holliday legends, and the Flat's legends. Officially, Doc's whole existence at Fort Griffin is summed up in the two entries in the court records. Edgar Rye, who arrived in 1876, doesn't mention him at all. Neither does Sallie Reynolds Mathews in *Interwoven*. And Doc had already become an epic figure by the time they compiled their memoirs. If he had attracted attention in the Flat, surely they would have said something.

Big Nose Kate's fire is mentioned in passing in Pat Jahn's brilliant biography of Doc. She traced the story not only to Fort Griffin, but to Caldwell and Hunnewell in Kansas. She also heard the story in connection with a completely different couple than Doc and Kate. In the end, she doesn't take it seriously.[30] The story remains clouded to this day.

---

[30]Jahns, pp. 111-112.

6

Judge Lynch
Takes a Hand

People like Doc Holliday and Lottie Deno were minor irritants in the overall scheme of things in the Flat. The horse thieves, rustlers and cutthroats in general were the real problem. And as the town between Government Hill and the Clear Fork grew rowdier, three factions emerged with a distinct interest in law enforcement.

The most important of these factions, of course, was the outlaws. After all, without them, there would have been no need for the other two. At times it was difficult to tell from one month to the next who belonged to the outlaws. Many frontier lawmen were themselves drifters and gunslingers. The sheriff who signed the wanted poster in one jurisdiction might be wanted in another jurisdiction.

The second faction was the local vigilance committee, referred to in Fort Griffin at various times as the Old Law Mob, the Tin-Hat Brigade, or simply the Vigilance Committee.[1] These were solid, respectable citizens

---

[1]The origins of these terms are obscure. "Old Law Mob" may refer to the ancient law of self-preservation, which C.L. Sonnichsen explained with such thoroughness and understanding in his introduction to *I'll Die Before I'll Run* (pp. 6-7). "Tin-Hat Brigade" is less clear. Joan Farmer, the gracious and knowledgeable

with family and property to defend, who sincerely believed the legal system couldn't—or wouldn't—take
adequate measures to protect them from the outlaws.
They were firm advocates of direct action, and many a
body swung from trees along the Clear Fork to attest
to that conviction.

Finally, there was the faction which firmly held that
judicial law, with all its imperfections, was infinitely
preferable to lynch law.

In a way, both groups were right and both were
wrong.

Even in the 19th Century, vigilantes were subject to
criticism, most of it coming from long-established and
peaceful communities in the East. And as true law
enforcement moved westward, the distaste for vigilance justice went with it. The image further suffered
with the 1940 publication and subsequent film of
Walter Van Tilburg Clark's *The Ox-Bow Incident* which
drew a chilling parallel with what was then going on in
Germany.[2]

But the fact was, the legal system did not work in
many places, and until something vaguely resembling
law and order could be established, the burden of
protection fell on ordinary citizens.

Edgar Rye served as justice of the peace, and as such
represented the legal system in Shackelford County.
Even so, he grasped the reality of the situation when
he wrote:

When it is understood that the honest, legitimate citizens

---

archivist in Albany, says local rumor has it that the committee members might
have put tin bands around their hats as they prepared to dispense frontier justice.
However, the organization itself was secret, so no one really seems to know. The
term was used in the 1870s, however, as we see from contemporary newspaper
accounts. "Vigilance Committee," of course, is self-explanatory.

[2]Norman V. Richards, *Cowboy Movies*, p. 39.

were in the minority and scattered over a large area, while the thieves, robbers and murderers were banded together and did not hestitate to testify falsely in court or waylay and kill witnesses to prevent conviction, the necessity to organize a Vigilance Committee to rid the community of these lawless characters when the law was impotent, at once becomes apparent.[3]

The rise of vigilance justice in the area seems to have coincided with the abandonment of Camp Cooper in 1861. With the military gone, there was no law and order, and cattlemen began having trouble with rustlers. To combat this, they apparently formed the first vigilance committee, known as the Old Law Mob, or more familiarly, by its initials O.L.M. Since those were the days before frontier journalism or heavy settlement, little is known about its organization or its workings.[4] We must rely on the memories of local citizens,

---

[3]Rye, p. 115. Rye himself is thought to have been connected to the vigilance committee.   [4]Grant, p. 86.

Edgar Rye. Courtesy of
author's collection.

recalling events that happened decades earlier, and secrets which they picked up by hearsay. But if the Old Law Mob was secretive in its methods, it made no secret of what it was about. Its victims were often found strung up to trees with the initials "O.L.M." pinned to them.[5]

Even the name of Collins Creek can be traced back to the O.L.M. Several stories have arisen concerning the circumstances, but they all point back to how a man named Collins met his end with the initials affixed to his body. John Chadbourne Irwin said Collins was shot after an anonymous letter accused him of stealing government mules from Camp Cooper. Don Biggers maintained he died "for purely social and commercial reasons" without elaborating.[6]

Perhaps the O.L.M. had reasons for doing Collins in. But the death of a lawyer named King[7] shows that toward the end, it had degenerated from a true vigilance committee into a bunch of gangsters out to settle personal vendettas.

It seems the wife of a rancher named Maxwell decided she wanted a divorce and engaged King to start the legal proceedings. According to Irwin, "Rumors had accused Mrs. Maxwell of trying to rid herself of her husband by foul means, and the lawyer was advised to leave immediately." When, after twenty-four hours, he was still in town, persons unknown decided to take action. A few days later, he was found hanging from a tree on the Clear Fork, with "O.L.M." pinned to his

[5]Joan Farmer in notes to Biggers, p. 89; Grant, p. 87; John Chadbourne Irwin to J.R. Webb.

[6]Irwin to Webb; Biggers, p. 41.

[7]Irwin to Webb; Grant (p. 86) calls him Fisch. Barbara A. Ledbetter (*Fort Belknap*, p. 87) says M.B. King was hanged on the Clear Fork by Hugh Harper, John Maxwell and Rufus Oliphant, adherents of Indian-hater John R. Baylor.

body. "I saw his remains, which were never buried, but tossed in a ravine,"[8] Irwin recalled.

Not long afterwards, the Old Law Mob seems to have faded into oblivion. By now, the military was well established at Fort Griffin, and with no civil government, post commanders extended their jurisdiction into the surrounding area. But the organization of Shackelford County put law enforcement outside of the military reservation into civilian hands. Since the Flat was really starting to grow, it wasn't long before the situation got too hot to handle.[9]

The Flat functioned as best it could for over a year, but killings continued unabated and so did robberies. Cattle theft was a thriving business too, particularly in view of the area's proximity to the Red River. A few days hard driving would take outlaws and their stolen stock into Indian Territory, and beyond the reach of normal legal channels. So what if the push to the border cost them a few head? It wasn't their cattle anyway. As if that weren't enough, some of the ranches in the area served as bases for prairie pirates.

The first hint that the average citizen was fed up came in the early part of 1876. Rye, who arrived in March, noted that it didn't take long to conclude "that there was trouble brewing between the unlawful denizens and the better element of the people."[10]

The "better element of the people" was represented by John Larn. By now, he was already well-established in the community. He had come to the area as a cowboy, and had gone to work for Joseph B. Mathews. Ultimately, he married into the family and set up a spread

---

[8]Irwin to Webb; Grant, p. 86.

[9]Sonnichsen, pp. 150-151; Irwin to Webb.

[10]Rye, p. 99.

of his own near the site of old Camp Cooper. In March 1874, he had been out horse hunting and had come upon a raiding party of Indians. Keeping cool, he managed to outride them until he reached the safety of his home.[11] His tough, no-nonsense attitude toward law and order and self-preservation made him a leader of the new vigilance movement which was beginning to form. Put quite simply, Sheriff Jacobs' efforts were not enough. New blood was needed. If anyone seemed the man to clean up Shackelford County, it was Larn. In the election of 1876, he became sheriff.[12]

Larn took office on April 18 and soon proved public confidence was well founded. Among his first acts was to appoint John Selman as his deputy.[13] Then, having obtained a warrant, they went after Shorty Collins, whom Rye called "an all-around horse thief, crook and murderer."[14]

Shorty had pretty much taken over the Flat, and together with Heck Thomas' South Texas cowboys, was running it to suit himself. Larn and Selman stopped them in front of Frankel's store on Griffin Avenue. They had apparently been drinking, and Shorty wasn't in any mood to deal with a lawman toting a warrant. So when Larn served it, he went for his gun. Selman had been watching for this, and before Shorty could clear his holster, he fell dead at Larn's feet.

For a moment, it looked like the cowboys would fight. Then Larn spoke up.

[11]Sonnichsen, pp. 154-155.

[12]Frances Mayhugh Holden, Lambshead, pp. 138-139.

[13]The name is sometimes rendered "Sillman." Selman himself appears to have pronounced it with an "i", although he always spelled it "Selman." Likewise, Larn has been written as Laren, Lorin and Laurens. His own signature is "John Larn" and his tombstone says "John M. Larn."

[14]Rye, p. 104.

John M. Larn. Courtesy, Old
Jail Art Center and Archive,
Albany, Texas.

"This is not your funeral, boys. This man Shorty is a
hardened criminal, and only got what is coming to
him. He threw in with your bunch to escape being
arrested. It is all right for you to stay with a friend, and
I would consider that you were white-livered curs if
you deserted a friend. But I know you do not wish to
shield a horse thief and a murderer."

Heck Thomas was willing to see it Larn's way, especially after the new sheriff offered to stand the
drinks.[15]

With Larn as sheriff, the Vigilance Committee got

---

[15]The version given appears in Rye, pp. 104-105. Leon C. Metz, in *John Selman,
Gunfighter* (pp. 62-63) seems to feel the conversation was largely a fabrication by
Rye. However, it is no more farfetched than many other conversations of that
period, regardless of the source. In his book, Metz accepts an account by Biggers
(p. 42), which may or may not have been based on the same incident. The sheriff
and deputy are not named, but are obviously Larn and Selman. The victim is
identified as "Hampton." According to Biggers, Hampton was walking across the
street when confronted by Larn and Selman. Apparently being slightly deaf, he
failed to heed Selman's command to put up his hands, with which the deputy
emptied his six-shooter at him.

busy. Ten days after he took office, the lead story of the Jacksboro *Frontier Echo*[16] was as follows:

MOB LAW!

Judge Lynch holds Court at Fort Griffin.[17]

Dispensation of Justice.

The *ECHO* is in receipt of special dispatches from Fort Griffin, Shackelford county, giving the particulars of the hanging of Houston Faught at that place by a body of vigilantes on the night of the 20th inst . . .

Faught was caught in the act of stealing a horse one night last week; shot, captured and conveyed to the military hospital at Fort Griffin for treatment. His wounds were slight, he was rapidly recovering, when, to prevent the possibility of his escape he was put under guard of some of the best citizens of the place. About 11 o'clock on the night of the 20th a party of mounted men, armed and disguised, suddenly made their appearance, arrested and disarmed the guard who they told that they (the maskers) had come to relieve Faught.

The maskers took the guard away from the building in which Faught was confined, then took him to the Clear Fork and hung him to a tree, after which they released the guard, restored to them their arms and told them to get out.

The following card was found pinned to Faught's clothing: "Horse thief No. 5, that killed and scalped that boy for Indian sign. Shall horse thieves rule the country? He will have company soon."

Thus ends the career of a man who has led a life of crime and created trouble wherever he sojourned. A few more of the same sort are left, but they will give Shackelford county a wide berth if they know when they are well off.

[16]Jacksboro *Frontier Echo*, Apr. 28, 1879.

[17]In such instances, "Judge Lynch" refers to lynch law, not to be confused with Judge John C. Lynch, prominent local citizen.

Elsewhere in the same story, editor G.W. Robson decried vigilance justice, but qualified it by saying, "...it seems as though no medicine will reach the case but blue whistlers or hemp. Twenty-six head of horses were recently stolen from one cattle ranch near Griffin, stock has been stolen from quite a number of citizens of the county, also from the Tonkawa Indians. The stealing of horses has become so frequent that the losers could not purchase fresh stock fast enough to satisfy the demands of the horse thief.

"The people have risen in their might and declared that thieves shall no longer rule the country."

One wonders where the military was when Faught was lynched. Although the story does not specify, presumably he had already been removed from the post hospital and taken into town under guard. It is hard to imagine the army letting something like that happen in its jurisdiction.

The new sheriff was apparently out of town and missed the proceedings. Larn had specifically been elected to deal with a gang of "cut-throats, robbers and cattle rustlers,"[18] who hung out in the Wichita Mountains near Fort Sill in the Indian Territory. Headed by Charley McBride, Bill English and Jim Townsend, they would sweep down through the Shackelford County area and back across the Red River before anyone could stop them. One of their rendezvous points in Fort Griffin was the shanty of Indian Kate and her daughter Mag, down by the Clear Fork at the end of Griffin Avenue.

One morning a cowboy riding in from the Mathews Ranch found the bodies of McBride, Townsend and a gang member named Brownlee hanging from trees

---

[18]Rye, p. 99.

along the Clear Fork bottoms. English had escaped to Kansas. Meanwhile, Bill Henderson, one of the worst members of the gang, and a man named Floyd had robbed and murdered a rancher in nearby Jones County, then taken off to Kansas and disappeared. Since Jones was joined to Shackelford for judicial purposes, Larn obtained a warrant and left in pursuit. On April 27, Town Marshal Bill Gilson got a telegram from Larn saying he had Henderson in Dodge City and was bringing him back. He arrrived in Griffin June 1, with both Henderson and Floyd in tow.[19]

The two outlaws didn't have long to wait. At the usual time of 11 p.m. the following night, a mob of about 50 men afoot and 20 more on horseback came to the jail in Albany. They disarmed the two guards and marched Henderson and Floyd up Hubbard Creek, where their bodies were found the next morning.

Commenting on the hangings, the *Frontier Echo* noted, "It is at best a deplorable state of affairs when Judge Lynch is called to preside, but so far, call them what you may, vigilants, tall tin hat fellows, or what you please, they have made no mistakes. There is nothing like knowing your man."[20]

There had been other lynchings than the two described thus far, and together they gave Fort Griffin a reputation as a lynch town. Other areas of the state were beginning to frown on this type of thing. In May, the McKinney *Enquirer* had reported that a petition was being circulated in the McKinney area, asking the legislature to set punishment for horse theft at flogging for the first offense, flogging and branding for the second, and hanging for the third.

Editor Robson hooted.

---

[19]Ibid., p. 99-101; Sonnichsen, pp. 154-155.
[20]Jacksboro *Frontier Echo*, June 9, 1876.

"Get out with your nonsense. What's the use of all that bother? Hang 'em first; then if they persist in their innocent amusement, cremate them. If that does not put the kibosh on 'em, we don't know what will."[21]

In fact, the same issue of the *Echo* had this item from Fort Griffin:

Court Proceedings on the
CLEAR FORK!
Judge Lynch Presiding

Special to THE ECHO
FORT GRIFFIN, TEXAS
May 7th, 1876

The notorious character known as "Reddy" of horse thief fame, was captured on the 2nd inst. at this place for horse stealing in Eastland county, and put in the military guard-house for safe keeping.

On Friday afternoon he was turned over to parties to be conveyed to Eastland county. Yesterday his body was found hanging to a tree three miles from here.[22]

The vigilantes were growing bolder. On June 23, they posted a notice between the telegraph office and Owen Donnelly's saloon, which was reprinted by the *Frontier Echo*:

NOTICE! NOTICE!

MORE TROUBLE!

MORE TROUBLE!

We've given notice that no prostitutes will be suffered to come among us. Several have come in the last few days. We know the parties who pursuaded them to come. When we strike, look out. We wait a little.

The prostitutes are less to blame than the men who bring

---

[21]Sonnichsen, pp. 155-156; W.C. Holden, "Law and Lawlessness on the Texas Frontier, 1876-1890," *SWHQ*, Oct. 1940, p. 197.

[22]Jacksboro *Frontier Echo*, May 12, 1876.

them and keep them but all will suffer. Leave or you are doomed—VIGILANCE.[23]

Of course the Shackelford County Vigilance Committee did not intend to go around hanging prostitutes when there were bigger problems at hand. Still the warning worked, and many of these people headed for calmer waters.[24] For the rougher element which didn't, there were always the trees on the Clear Fork.

Given John Larn's nerve and determination, most of these lynchings could not have taken place without his connivance, if not his active participation. This would have been strictly in violation of the law he was sworn to uphold. But as Rye grudgingly admitted, "During the first six months of his term Laren [sic] did more to quell lawlessness than any man who served the people as sheriff, before or since his time."[25]

Phin Reynolds added, "The hangings and killings of the ones accused of stealing had a good effect in stopping thieving in this country. After this time, there was less stealing here than anywhere I know of."[26]

Even so, the area around the Flat still had its moments. Some of it was caused by drink, some by economic factors or social problems, and some through sheer meanness.

Drink and social prejudice were responsible for a near disaster at the fort proper in October 1876, when it was occupied by black troops. The soldiers had just sat down to their evening meal when a drunken buffalo hunter stormed into the mess hall, pistol in each hand, and ordered them to get up and back out of the door one at a time. The troops followed his suggestion, and

[23]Ibid., June 30, 1876.
[24]Herbert M. Hart, *Old Forts of the Southwest*, p. 147.
[25]Rye, p. 106.   [26]P.W. Reynolds to J.R. Webb, Webb Papers.

when the last one had left, the hunter went to the door
and told them the first one back in would get his head
shot off.

The incident was reported to the company captain,
who ordered a lieutenant to form a firing squad, kill
the hunter and retake the hall. By that time, word had
filtered down the hill to Larn. Before the squad moved
in, he got the captain's permission to handle the matter.
Larn talked the hunter out, marched him down the hill
and threw him into a vacant shack to sleep it off. To
keep the hunter confined, he propped a log against the
door. But the prisoner wasn't ready to sleep, and tore
up the floor boards and built a fire. The flames spread
to the tinder dry building itself, which was soon engulfed. Trapped inside by Larn's log, the hunter was
overcome by fire and smoke. The sheriff managed to
drag him out before he sustained any serious injury.
By now, the hunter was cold sober, so Larn sent him on
his way.[27]

As stated earlier, some of the area ranches were
headquarters for cattle and horse thieves. One of these
was the Millet Ranch in nearby Throckmorton County.
This was part of a ranching empire run by several
brothers, which ranged from South Texas on up as far
as Idaho. The ranch in Throckmorton County was
headed up by the oldest brother, Alonzo Millet, who
hired the toughest men he could find.[28]

Newt Jones worked for the Millets from September
1876 to June 1877. At the time, Billy Bland was trail
boss. Jones called him "a desperate character, but a
good man in a way. He was always good to me and

---

[27]Grant, pp. 77-78.
[28]Frances Mayhugh Holden, *Lambshead*, p. 141.

straight in every way when I was around." Even so, Bland was a hard case, as were his ranch hand cronies Billie Gray, Charlie Reed and Jack Lyons. "They were burning cattle [altering brands], I am sure, but I never knew whose," Jones recalled.[29] It is very unlikely Alonzo Millet knew of their illegal activities. He had hired tough men for a tough job, and as far as he knew, they were serving him well.

Then, on January 19, 1877, the *Frontier Echo* reported:

SHOOTING BEE AT
Fort Griffin
Two dead, Others dieing

Yesterday morning news reached us that a shooting scrape occurred Wednesday night in Donley & Carroll's saloon or dancehouse at Fort Griffin, in which one man, a stranger in the place, was killed instantly and Billy Bland, a cowboy; Lieut. Myers, late of the 10th Cavalry, and a Mr. Jeffries, County Attorney of Shackelford county were wounded. The cause of the shooting or who done it we could not learn.

LATER—We since here that Lieut. Myers died yesterday morning and Bland last night.[30]

According to Charlie Reed, Bland had started shooting up the saloon "just for fun." Deputy Bill Cruger shot Bland. Bland was still able to return fire and wounded Cruger slightly. Then someone shouted, "I order you to surrender," to which Reed shouted, "I order you to get." The other person ran out, and Reed never saw who it was.

Reed ran out the front door and headed toward Clampett's wagon yard, where he had left his horse. But a crowd was gathering there, so he climbed the back fence and left town on foot. He walked twelve

---

[29]Newton Josephus Jones to J.R. Webb, Webb Papers.
[30]Jacksboro *Frontier Echo*, Jan. 19, 1877.

miles to one of the ranch camps at Mackenzie Crossing, where Newt Jones hid him until morning, when he recovered his horse and took off.

Back at Donley & Carroll's, the "stranger," identified as Dan Barron, and former Lt. J.W. Myers, both bystanders, had been hit probably by Bland's random gunplay. Barron was dead and Myers was dying. The county attorney, William Jeffries, who had participated in the fight, was badly wounded. When Jones saw him at a picnic the following summer, he was still confined to a wheelchair.[31]

Charlie Reed disappeared. Jones was a Ranger when he saw him again, nearly a year later. "I did not arrest him, for I feared if I did, we would send him back to Albany, and he would be killed by the Vigilance Committee (or mob). He did say to me, 'Newt, how many men do you have with you? You could make it pretty hard on me,' to which I replied, 'I helped you get away once, and I would not arrest you now to be turned over to the mob to be killed.'"[32] Reed left Texas, and Jones later heard rumors that he had been lynched in Nebraska for killing a man.

Soon after the saloon fight in Griffin, Jones recalled "John Larn, the Sheriff of Shackelford County, resigned his office, and it was generally believed in the community that he was in sympathy with Bland in this fight, resented the killing, and resigned in protest over the killing of Bland."[33]

---

[31]Newton Josephus Jones to J.R. Webb. Lt. J.W. Myers, 10th Cavalry, had been dismissed from the service by order of court martial convened at Fort Griffin on May 27, 1875. (H.C. Smith Papers). Other records refer to attorney Robert A. Jefress. At this date the conflict cannot be resolved.

[32]Newton Josephus Jones to J.R. Webb.

[33]Ibid.

Larn and Bland were, in fact, friends. With this single shooting at Donley & Carroll's, an old order began to die, and a new one rose to take its place. The stage was set for a tragedy that would rip the Flat inside out and bring pain to the county's most respected families.

7

The Larn Affair

In Shackelford County, the name "John Larn" brings an immediate reaction. "That's still a pretty sore subject around here," a park ranger at Fort Griffin told me in July 1986. Few men who were not national figures have caused so much lasting unhappiness to so many people in so short a time as Larn. Few men have had such complicated and contradictory personalities. Few have been shrouded in so much mystery.

Nobody really knows where Larn came from. He told Phin Reynolds he had been a newsboy on a train out of Mobile, Alabama, had run away from home and gone west. "He told me that he came to Griffin from Trinidad, Colorado. Said that a fellow for whom he worked would not pay him so he took a horse and left. The man followed him on a mule to the Patterson Bottom above Rocky Ford, Colorado, and rode up to him with a gun in his hand and said, 'I've got you.' Larn said that he then drew his gun and killed him."[1]

Sophie Poe and Edgar Rye believed he came to Griffin from Dodge City. "He was a man of strong and pleasant personality—typical cowboy," wrote Mrs. Poe, whose second-hand description reflected the feelings of those who knew him.[2]

---

[1]John Larn to P.W. Reynolds, Webb Papers.
[2]Sophie Poe, *Buckboard Days*, p. 88; Rye, p. 103.

The 1870 census for Fort Griffin lists him as a stock-raiser from Alabama, 21 years old, living in the household of Susan Reynolds Newcomb, together with her brother, Ben Reynolds.[3]

Regardless of where he came from, it was generally agreed he had polish, culture, Southern civility and talent. Judge A.A. Clarke called him "one of the best mannered men."[4] That may have been. But by the time he drifted into Griffin, about 1870, he had at least two killings to his credit. One involved the horse-owner from Colorado, whom Larn supposedly shot in self-defense. But Johnny Shannessy, a cutthroat who knew his own kind, maintained it was cold-blooded murder. The second involved a sheriff in New Mexico, whom Larn admitted gunning down, although once again, he claimed self-defense.[5]

In fact, John Larn was a killer.

Larn's real notoriety in Griffin began in July 1871, when Bill Hayes had a herd of cattle to be driven to Colorado. Hayes himself was a ruthless character, and he wanted a ruthless trail boss to run his herd. He hired Larn. The remainder of the summer was spent rounding up the cattle. On September 10, Hayes tallied the herd, after which Larn headed it down toward Fort Concho for brand inspection before turning northwest to Trinidad.[6]

But for reasons of his own, Larn bypassed Fort Concho and headed on toward Horsehead Crossing on

[3]Holden, *Lambshead*, p. 128.

[4]Miss Ollie Clarke, Nail Papers.

[5]Dick Shaughnessy (i.e., Johnny Shannesy) to P.W. Reynolds, Webb Papers; Holden, *Lambshead*, pp. 130-131.

[6]Larn's association with Bill Hayes, the subsequent mobbing of the Hayes outfit and the Reynolds reaction are drawn from Holden, *Lambshead*, pp. 129-133; P.W. Reynolds to J.R. Webb; and John Chadbourne Irwin, the latter two in the Webb Papers.

the Pecos River. Reaching the crossing, he murdered two well-mounted young Mexicans, threw their bodies into the river, and seized their horses and gear. Later, in New Mexico, Larn and his point rider killed a Mexican shepherd. There seems to have been no reason for these killings, other than a dislike Larn had for Mexicans.

Hayes met the herd in Colorado and was pleased with the fact that it had grown substantially, even though there was no logical explanation for that growth. The cattle were taken to Trinchera Peak near Trinidad to winter, while Hayes tried to get a good price. But the market was down, and with branding time approaching on the Clear Fork, he was still unable to sell the herd. He gave Larn his power of attorney and sent him back to Griffin along with Bill Bush and another cowboy.

Bill Hayes struggled in Colorado another eighteen months or so, until he lost his herd to creditors. Meanwhile, Larn and Bush had parlayed their power of attorney over Hayes' Clear Fork holdings into a nice little herd of their own. In fact, when Hayes finally returned to Texas in the summer of 1873, he found Larn claiming rights to his brands. Bush realigned himself and threw in with Hayes, but by now, Larn was in control. When Bill Hayes, his brother John, and Bush put together another herd for a drive to Fort Sill, Larn swore out a warrant against them on charges of cattle theft. Then he, Acting Sheriff Riley Carter and a squad of black cavalry from Fort Griffin set off in pursuit.

The Hayes brothers, Bush and five other cowboys were still rounding up cattle for the drive, and were camped at Bush Knob, in Throckmorton County, some thirty miles or so north of Griffin. Exactly what happened there is uncertain, but the Hayes boys, Bush and four others were killed. One member of the group, whom John C. Irwin called "a boy," was turned loose. It was all done under the cloak of legality, with the assistance of the Army. Irwin later pointed out that this was during Reconstruction and the Army had a lot of leeway about that sort of thing. Even so, the incident bothered Phin and George Reynolds, particularly since Larn had ingratiated himself with their in-laws.

The in-laws in question were the Mathews. In 1867, Joseph B. Mathews' daughter, Lucinda Elizabeth, had married George Reynolds. In 1872, while Bill Hayes was still struggling against his creditors in Colorado, Larn went to work as a foreman for Mathews. His good looks, courtly manners and overall sense of responsibility soon won the admiration of the second daughter, Mary Jane, and they made plans to marry.[7]

Although Larn had yet to engineer the deaths of the Hayes outfit, the Reynolds boys were already uneasy over the killings on the trail to Colorado. They counseled Joe B. against the match. Mathews himself had misgivings and, together with his wife, advised Mary against it. The fact was, they knew nothing about Larn.[8]

Mary Mathews was adamant. The wedding went off without a hitch, and Joe Mathews gave his new son-in-law five hundred head of cattle. This herd, together with the cattle he was skimming from the Hayes holdings, gave Larn enough independence to set up his own spread. He took his bride across the Clear Fork to the ruins of old Camp Cooper, where he built his "Honeymoon Cottage" from the stones of the abandoned mili-

---

[7]Holden, *Lambshead*, p. 89.
[8]Rye, p. 104; Interview with Joan Farmer.

tary buildings. With a sense of beauty and design, another trait that bespoke an above average background, he laid out a garden. Here, some humor came into play. The flower beds were shaped like diamonds, hearts and spades.[9]

It was perhaps about this time that Larn teamed up with John Selman. The latter went back earlier in the area, if pioneers in a new territory can be said to go back very far. He had come with his family to the settlement of Fort Davis during the War Between the States. Among his neighbors was Jasper N. deGraffenreid, whose sister, Edna, he would marry.[10] Selman learned the butcher's trade from deGraffenreid, a trade he would use during his association with Larn. In 1869, the two brothers-in-law took their families to New Mexico, where the Selmans stayed a year before moving back to the Clear Fork and Fort Griffin.[11]

Never were two men more oddly matched. Selman was ten years Larn's senior. His black hair was sprinkled with grey. He had a downcast look and was generally unkempt.[12] Next to him, Larn appeared—as indeed he was—princely. He was described as "fine looking, of good address, good nerve and a splendid marksman." His marriage "gave him influence and social standing."[13]

From all accounts, Larn was genuinely in love with his wife. Mrs. A.A. Clarke said there was no more thoughtful and considerate husband. Seventy years later, as he approached the century mark, Newt Jones recalled that Larn and Selman put down their share of liquor during Billy Bland's drinking bouts at the Millet

[9]Interview with Joan Farmer.
[10]Metz, *John Selman*, pp. 25-26, 39.
[11]Ibid., pp. 39-40.
[12]Nail Papers.
[13]Galveston *News*, July 13, 1878.

Ranch.[14] Of Selman, that was probably true. But the bulk of the evidence shows Larn to have been a total abstainer who neither smoked nor drank, although he freely associated with those who did. Even Phin Reynolds called Larn "a bad man, but most likeable."[15]

So this was the partnership. Larn was young and respectable, stayed sober, and went home at night. Selman was older, a debauchee who drank to excess and publicly consorted with Hurricane Minnie Martin, the prostitute.[16] But Selman's problems were largely social rather than legal, until Larn came along. His was the sinister influence that turned Selman from an ordinary reprobate into a gunfighter and an outlaw.[17]

John Larn prospered, but it always seemed to be at someone else's expense. For awhile, in 1874, he allowed a man named Bryant to run cattle on his Camp Cooper spread. Then one of Larn's hands killed Bryant under suspicious circumstances. Since the victim had no known friends or relatives, Larn kept his cattle "without administration."[18]

Still, Larn's prestige was such that no one questioned him, his methods or his motives. His herd was doing well enough to allow him to sell cattle to contractors. He and Mary had a son, Will, and by all accounts, he was the perfect doting father. In 1876, Larn moved his family directly across the Clear Fork to a new house, one which he designed himself. The house was a masterpiece. Even today, after five or six renovations, a visitor cannot help but be impressed by Larn's architectural skill and sense of style.[19]

---

[14]Newton Josephus Jones to J.R. Webb.

[15]Webb Papers.

[16]Nail Papers.

[17]Metz, *John Selman*, p. 52.

[18]Galveston *News*, July 13, 1878.

[19]Miscellaneous notes, Nail Papers; Holden, *Lambshead*, p. 135; Metz, *John Selman*, pp. 54-55.

Initially, there was a large, glassed-in cupola which was later removed. Local legend has it that it served as a watchtower. But the present owner, Mrs. J.C. Putnam does not believe it, and Leon Metz points out that all of the better homes of the period had them.[20] Perhaps the most outstanding feature of the house is a magnificent wooden medallion, also designed by Larn, in the middle of the dining room ceiling. Before the house was electrified, a kerosene lamp hung down from the center of the medallion. Although it has never been dismantled for examination, it is said to contain more than two hundred separate pieces of wood.

Here Larn ran his growing ranch and held court among an increasingly tough group of cowhands. Among them was Selman, who was his neighbor at the Rock Ranch, two miles up the Clear Fork, as well as his employee, business associate, and unofficial deputy when Larn became sheriff.[21]

There was one blight on John and Mary Larn's happiness during this period. On March 24, 1875, they had a second son, whom they named Joseph. The baby lived not quite six months, dying on September 17. The grief-stricken father buried him in the yard of his new home, and erected a fine headstone.[22]

As we have seen, Larn had a reasonably successful career as sheriff, until he chose to end it after the death of Billy Bland. The killing left a sour taste in his mouth. And since his deputy, Bill Cruger was involved, it apparently created a public breach between Larn and the forces of decency. In this case, the forces of decency were the Shackelford County Vigilance Committee.

20Interview with Mrs. J.C. Putnam; Metz, *John Selman*, p. 55.

21Metz, *John Selman*, p. 52.

22Holden, *Lambshead*, p. 115; tombstone of Joseph Larn, old Larn Place, Throckmorton County, Texas.

With Bland dead, Alonzo Millet replaced him as foreman with a man identified only as "Captain Young," who was as straight as his predecessor had been crooked. "He was a good man, had no use for men who were doing like [Bland's friends] were doing," Newt Jones recalled.[23]

The end was nearing for the Bland group, which included Larn, Selman, Billie Gray and Jack Lyons. They began to worry about the Vigilance Committee, and those who lived at Millet's Stone Ranch Camp would ride out into the mountains to spend the night. Finally, Millet and Young gave notice that the Vigilantes would leave the gang alone if they calmed down. Lyons and Gray left the country. Larn and Selman, with families and property, stayed behind.[24]

Left to their own devices, they secured appointments as deputy inspectors of hides and animals for the county. Joe B. Mathews and Frank Conrad co-signed their bonds. Hide inspection could be lucrative, particularly if a trail boss was gullible enough to pay, or in a hurry to get through with minimal delays. In fact, it was made into a substantial racket by those crooked enough. And Larn and Selman were definitely crooked enough.

The inspector's job not only involved inspection of herds, but of butchers as well. Here, Selman's earlier experiences with Jasper deGraffenreid were helpful. In addition, he and Larn received a contract to furnish meat for the military at Fort Griffin.[25] The contract required three beeves a day, and the Larn-Selman part-

[23]Newton Josephus Jones to J.R. Webb, Webb Papers.

[24]Ibid.

[25]Lieutenant G.W. Campbell to Major John B. Jones, Feb. 26, 1878, in AGO RG 401-1159, Frontier Battalion, Letters, 1878, hereinafter referred to as "Letters"; Metz, *John Selman*, pp. 72-73.

nership always managed to meet the terms. Oddly enough, the sizes of their herds seemed to remain the same, while neighboring ranchers noticed their cattle were disappearing.[26]

There was no question that Larn and his gang were stealing cattle to meet their contracts. But an encounter between Larn and John C. Irwin shows why people were so loath to do anything about it.

Irwin was having a particularly bad year. He had good cattle, but there was a drought and he had no grass. Early one morning, he noticed a disturbance in his pasture, and saw Larn personally rounding up and driving off part of his herd. Aware of the man's reputation for killing, he kept quiet.

A few days later, Irwin was in Fort Griffin when Larn came up, put his arm around his shoulder, and asked, "How are things, Johnny?"

"I've got all those cattle out there, and I haven't got money to buy feed for them. Things are mighty bad. I just don't know what I am going to do," Irwin replied. "I'll tell you what I am going to do for you, Johnny. I am going to give you $100—just to help you along."

With that, Larn handed him a $100 bill. Both of them knew the situation, and that Irwin's cattle losses to Larn far exceeded $100. But this was cash, and Irwin was glad to get it. "And somehow, I never could really dislike Larn after that," he said.[27]

Hard cash, generosity on call, family connections and a reputation for cold-blooded murder. These were the things that allowed John Larn to get away with so much for so long. In particular, the reputation as a killer allowed him a lot of leeway. For the longer Larn

---

[26]Rye, p. 106.
[27]J.W. George to Robert Nail, quoting John Chadbourne Irwin, Nail Papers.

lived in the Fort Griffin area, the darker the stories grew.

In the spring of 1878, he hired two stonemasons to build a rock fence around his property for $500. He paid them $100 in advance with the balance due on completion. When the project was finished, they simply disappeared. About two weeks later, a body, decayed beyond recognition, was pulled from the Clear Fork near Fort Griffin. Another was pulled out downriver in Stephens County.[28] Rumors spread that Larn had killed the two masons in order to avoid paying their balance. But Phin Reynolds never accepted the story. "I have heard that one of them was seen after that [killing] was supposed to have occurred. Although Larn was a pretty hard character, I do not believe that he did it."[29]

Whether or not Larn killed the stonemasons, there were too many rumors floating around, and too little was being done about them. Although Company B of the Texas Rangers' Frontier Battalion was stationed at nearby Camp Sibley, the commanding officer, Captain G.W. Arrington, was not acting promptly enough to suit some citizens. In fact, Bill Cruger, now sheriff, had already complained to the Adjutant General's Office in Austin that he was having trouble getting cooperation from Arrington.[30] Consequently, he was replaced by Lieutenant G.W. Campbell, who perhaps would get things done.

Campbell did. In February 1878, several citizens swore out a warrant charging Larn and Selman with "stealing cattle and killing them for beef," and Campbell prepared to serve it. He gathered up another

[28]Galveston *News*, July 13, 1878.
[29]P.W. Reynolds to J.R. Webb.
[30]Annual report of the AGO, fiscal year ending Aug. 31, 1878.

Ranger and twelve local deputies and rode out to Larn's place. There, he told the others to wait while he went into the house. According to Irwin, who was a member of the posse, Campbell was inside for about an hour, and when he came out, he was accompanied by Larn, John and Tom Selman, and a henchman named Tom Curtis. Seeing the group gathered around, Larn lost his composure for perhaps the first time in his life, and "started cursing our entire bunch of deputies and dared them to come through the yard. The ranger remonstrated with him, but to no avail. Well, we didn't go through the yard, but we did go around it and to the river, just below his house, where we fished out cow hides with grappling hooks. This was done in the presence of Larn and the Selmans. These hides had various brands on them, but we found none with the brands of either Selman or Larn. Larn claimed they had been planted there to frame him."[31]

In his report to Major John B. Jones, commander of the Frontier Battalion, Campbell wrote that the group had "found six beef hides in the bed of the Clear Fork, none in their own brands (Laurn & Sellmans)."[32]

There may have been more than one effort to drag the river for hides. A story has it that as dragging was going on one day, Larn rode up unexpectedly. Sitting on horseback on the bank above, where he could observe without being seen, he called down, "Any man who pulls that line up will be a dead man." Nobody pulled and everybody moved out.[33]

Regardless of how many draggings were made, Camp-

---

[31]John Chadbourne Irwin to J.R. Webb; Campbell to Jones, Feb. 26, 1878, in Letters.
[32]Campbell to Jones, Feb. 26, 1878; ibid.
[33]Bob Green to Robert Nail, Nail Papers.

bell's visit had one result. Larn and Selman were ordered to report to Fort Griffin under arrest. Once there, "a compromise was made; and the parties were released."[34] R.A. Hutchison, the other Ranger in Campbell's search party, was less charitable. He told Newt Jones only one hide was identified, and its owner had been offered $50 to keep quiet. As a former Vigilante, Larn knew too much about too many people, who couldn't afford to face him in court.[35]

The whole drama now took on an unreal combination of overconfidence and extreme caution. Larn and Selman seemed to feel they could get away with anything. Yet the time had also come to deal with any potential witnesses. Their principal antagonists were grangers, small landholders who eked out a subsistance living on 160-acre tracts of the old Comanche reservation.[36] While they barely produced enough crops or livestock to support themselves, their presence was enough to interfere with the plans of an up-and-coming cattleman-outlaw like Larn. Larn's family connections might protect him from open accusaions by the large landholders, but not from the grangers.

Larn and Selman now had about sixteen men under their command. With these men, carrying the most modern weapons, they took to night riding. In his semi-monthly report to Major Jones, Ranger Sergeant J.E. Van Riper, acting in Campbell's stead, stated, "A feud has existed for several months between Jno. M. Laurn, Jno. H. Sellman & party, and the farmers, on account of the unlawful killing and using of stock; and finally the killing of stock in general of the farmers, on the range and elsewhere through malitious [sic] intents,

---

[34]Campbell to Jones, Feb. 26, 1878, in Letters.
[35]Newton Josephus Jones to J.R. Webb.
[36]Holden, *Lambshead*, p. 117.

and serious threats to exterminate and drive the farmers from the country; the farmers not being able to
receive redress by law have taken up arms in defense
of their lives and property, both parties travil [sic] the
country in squads, well armed—trouble is hourly
expected."[37]

In March, the Rangers got a break. Hurricane Bill
Martin had been arrested in San Antonio on a warrant
from Shackelford County, charging him with assault
with intent to murder. He had formerly been employed
by the Vigilance Committee to tie the ropes of lynch
victims, and later to cut them down and dispose of the
bodies. Now, he was ready to talk. Larn and Selman
saw this could involve them. To aggravate their problems, their own relations with their erstwhile Vigilante
associates were becoming strained.[38]

Hurricane Bill arrived back in Albany on April 1, in
the custody of Rangers J.E. Hines and E.W. Jordan.
Campbell was jubilant. Here was his chance, not only
to nail Larn and Selman, but to clean up Shackelford
County entirely. He wrote to Jones:

> [Bill] has spoken very plainly to Mr. Hines, that he has been
> with the parties that are now persecuting him, "the *Vigilance
> Mob*" [Campbell's emphasis] of Shackelford County—in the

[37]Sergeant J.E. Van Riper to Jones, June 15, 1878, in Letters. This is the extent of
the signed report presently (July, 1988) on file in Austin. In the summer of 1944,
when he was sorting through the Adjutant General's files, C.L. Sonnichsen found
a much longer copy. In that one, Van Riper not only gave the information included
in this chapter, but also wrote that several bodies had recently turned up in the
Clear Fork and that he did not trust the coroner's verdict. He noted Larn had
openly threatened five persons, including himself and Campbell, and said the
Rangers were "nightly expectant of a raid." Finally, he told Jones he believed the
Ranger mail was being intercepted in Fort Griffin, and said henceforth he would
send his correspondence from Breckenridge. Sonnichsen copied the letters and
provided duplicates to J.R. Webb. These are presently in the Webb Papers at
Hardin-Simmons University.

[38]Holden, *Lambshead*, pp. 149-150; Metz, *John Selman*, pp. 78-80; Newton Josephus
Jones to J.R. Webb.

most of their *Cut throat* activities, of killing and hanging done
in Shackleford and adjoining Counties, Committed in the
last four or five years. He tells Mr. Hines that he does not
wish to give in his testimony or turn "states evidence," to
screen, or, protect himself in any way or to elude justice, in
the hands of a *just* law—but—that he does wish to have each,
and every one of these, *blood thirsty*, and Cut throat, "Tin
Hat Committee" to be checked in their Murderous Career,
and justice and *punishment*, meted to each and every one impli-
cated—to the *full* extent of the *Law*—He further tells Mr
Hines that, in case, his, testimony will not be accepted, he
will give the names of a sufficient number of Good and
reliable Citizens of this Country, that were *"eye witnesse[s]"* to
numbers of the atrocious, and inhuman, deeds performed
by this Vigilance Committee, and all that these witnesses
wish is *protection*. And that he Can, himself show the skeletons
of upwards of seven Victims of this *"Terrible Mob,"* foully
murdered in the past few years.—He further tells Mr Hines,
that he will give the names of all these parties; at the setting
of the next District Court, at Albany in Shackleford County,—and, that he will go and point out the *Identical parties*, that
did the dark deeds in this Country.—I think that I can
procure other witnesses, who will give evidence in these
Cases, that will corroborate with his! He is, or seems to be
afraid of this party, and that he may be *mobbed*,—to prevent
his testimony against them.—There are men in Shackleford,
and adjoining Counties that will come up and give their
evidence when these parties are arrested.—to my Opinion,
they are afraid to say anything in regards to these Cases,
until they are sure of protection. I [s]hall not act in the affair
until I hear from you, only to find out parties that I can use
as witnesses in these cases. I have left four men at Albany,
Shackleford County, to see that Martin is not taken out, and
put out of the way before Court. Should like to hear from
you, immediately as to what you think of this—and hope
that you could be at the District Court—*for if anything is done,
there will be no County Officers left to Conduct Court* [Author's
emphasis]—there is no jail at Albany and there is already
thirteen men under guard there. I think it will require a
good many men, to put this through properly,—I think that

Major John B. Jones,
Commander of the Frontier
Battalion Texas Rangers.
Courtesy, Texas State
Archives.

the parties, or at least the most of them, can be arrested at
the Court House; at the setting of the Court. If Martin will
do what he says he will, and I have not the least doubt to
Suspicion Else; no one has any suspicion of this, neither will
they find it out until we can secure them all."[39]

This widespread involvement of the county's leading
citizens gave Larn and Selman a much-needed breather.
Campbell's letter was intercepted in the Fort Griffin
post office. Faced with a common threat, the Vigilantes
and their backers went into action. Judge J.R. Fleming
dashed off a letter of his own to Governor R.B. Hubbard, accusing Campbell of grandstanding. Judge C.K.
Stribling also wrote. Hubbard gave the word to Adjutant General William Steele, who passed it on to Major
Jones. On May 7, Jones wrote Campbell that he would
probably be discharged from the service by the end of
the month, and the company reduced to a sergeant, a
corporal and six men. He added he hoped to personally

---

[39]Campbell to Jones, Apr. 3, 1878, in Letters.

visit the unit, and told Campbell to prepare a list of his preferences for those who would remain. Eleven days later, Jones sent another letter, saying Campbell's dismissal and the reduction of the unit were due to drains on Ranger finances at El Paso and elsewhere. He said his visit would probably be postponed until the middle of June, and told Campbell to leave Sergeant Van Riper in charge. He named Hines and two others to be retained, and told Campbell to use his discretion in picking the rest. One of those Campbell chose was Newt Jones.[40]

The situation was rapidly deteriorating. The Galveston *News* reported that "a Granger living within half a mile of [Larn's] place went out late in the afternoon to hunt his calves, and he has not been heard of since.

"This, with the disapperance of the two men [the stonemasons], and facts above recited, terrified the Grangers so that they ceased to work their crops, kept close in their houses, and would not even go to their cow-pens to milk; sending their wives out to transact all their business that was attended to. But few of them undressed themselves at nights . . . for fear of an attempt to mob. They were trying to sell their places, improved river valley land, with fine growing crops, for a pittance to get away on."[41]

For his part, Campbell was outraged at the shabby treatment he and his men had received for doing their duty. He was particularly hurt over rumors that they had been dishonorably discharged. On June 16, he wrote Major Jones, pointing out that several grangers had already abandoned their homes. Those who re-

40Jones to Campbell, May 7, 18, 1878, in Letters; Holden, *Lambshead,* pp. 149-150; Metz, *John Selman,* pp. 80-81.
41Galveston *News,* July 13, 1878.

mained did so primarily because they believed Jones would personally take charge and straighten the mess out.

Although he was under immense political pressure in Austin, Jones was a near legendary figure in the Clear Fork area from his exploits in the Indian Wars. Mentioning this, Campbell said the people "are after me every day wanting to know what to do, and when you will be up, as I had told them that if they would keep quiet until you arrived that the troubles would be stopped. You have no idea how bad your presence is needed here, at the present time, and how the citizens look to you and will flock to you for relief. If I have asked the question and within the last week, it has been asked me fifty times when you would be up. I have been telling them 'not to be rash and get themselves into trouble for there are too many [outlaws] for a few men to undertake to do anything with, besides they are well armed' and do not stay home at nights from what I understand.

"Major: in regards to the company, some parties have circulated the news over the country that this company was *Dishonorably Discharged* [Campbell's emphasis] from the service. I would much rather have stayed until you came up *without Pay* than as it is, on account of bringing these parties to justice, as for my wanting to remain in the service I was not nor am not anxious: only to have stayed long enough to see this thing ferrited [sic] out, and justice done to all parties[;] then I would have been satisfied and until this thing is done, I am not satisfied."[42]

Within a week of Campbell's letter, it was all over.

---

[42]Campbell to Jones, June 16, 1878, typescript in Webb Papers.

Larn was dead and Selman was on the run. It happened
this way:

A granger named A.J. Lancaster failed to return
home one night. His wife went to Cruger, who sent
out a search party under Deputy Jim Draper. The next
morning he was found, hidden in the brush along the
river, with a gunshot wound. He told the authorities
Larn and Selman had chased him along the Clear Fork
for several miles, and had opened fire as he dashed over
the river bank.

Lancaster was not seriously wounded, but had been
afraid of returning home, since he felt it would have
exposed his family to danger. After assuring his wife
that he was all right, he and another granger, William
Brisky, went into Albany and swore out a complaint
stating that "John Selman, John M. Larn, Thomas Curtis, John Gross, Thomas Selman, _____ Thistle and
Jimmy Herrington of Throckmorton County (a County
attached to this Co. for judicial purposes) diverse times
of late have threatened to do some serious bodily hurt
to the persons of deponents and that deponents fear
that the said John Selman, John M. Larn, Thomas
Curtis, Thomas Selman, _____ Thistle and Jimmy
Herrington will carry their said threats into execution,
unless restrained therefrom by due course of law."
On June 21, 1878, Justice of the Peace Edgar Rye issued
warrants for their arrest.[43]

Bill Cruger intended to have a quick arrest with
little or no gunplay. He rounded up a posse and rode
out to Larn's place in the early morning darkness. The
approaches were covered. No one was to enter or

[43]Shackelford County, Justice of the Peace Court, Precinct 1, Cause No. 26,
depositions, warrants, coroner's inquests, June 21-24, 1878, hereinafter cited as
"Larn Docket"; Rye, p. 107; Holden, Lambshead, p. 151.

leave. A little after sunrise, Larn stepped out with a milking pail. Cruger and several deputies followed him down the steep river bank toward the cowpens. There, Cruger called out that he had a warrant for his arrest. Larn unbuckled his gunbelt and handed it over. He was calm. He thought the order came from Fort Griffin, where he had enough friends to cover for him. "When he saw that the warrant was from the Court at Albany," Phin Reynolds recalled, "he trembled and said that he would not have surrendered had he have know[n] that the warrant was from the Albany Court."[44]

In fact, Larn felt there was a strong possibility of being lynched on the way to town. He asked for a gun to fight it out. The request was denied. Actually, the posse wasn't sure what to do with him. Most had been friends and associates at some point or another, and Larn's record as sheriff had been admirable. In a moment of panicky bravado, Larn himself made the decision for them. He informed them that if he ever got away, they were all dead men. Every man in the posse knew he meant it. From that moment on, John Larn's fate was sealed.[45]

To avoid a possible lynching, he demanded that Mary, Will and a hired hand accompany him. When they came out, he is said to have sat Will in his lap and asked him if he knew the members of the posse. When the boy said he did, Larn told him to remember them.

Larn was handcuffed and boosted onto a horse. Then his legs were tied down. "We have got the nest egg," Deputy Dave Barker remarked.[46] Once Larn was in

---

[44]P.W. Reynolds to J.R. Webb.

[45]Metz, *John Selman*, p. 87; interview with Joan Farmer; Galveston *News*, July 13, 1878.

[46]Rye, p. 108; quote from P.W. Reynolds to J.R. Webb, citing Ben Reynolds, a member of the posse.

Albany, they planned to get Selman. No one was really concerned about the others named in the warrant.

The procession passed through Fort Griffin, where Mary stopped long enough to secure the services of a young lawyer, John Wray. Then she followed the posse into Albany, and took a room at the Shields House, the local hotel.[47] Henry Herron took Larn to Charley Rainboldt's blacksmith shop, where leg irons were riveted on.[48] Then he was taken to the picket hut which served Albany as a makeshift jail.

John Selman's sordid lifestyle had saved his life. Unlike Larn, whose activities were primarily confined to cattle theft and murder, Selman had a wide spectrum of friends in the Fort Griffin underworld. Even before the posse headed toward Larn's house, word had started filtering through as to what was going to happen. Hurricane Minnie Martin secured a horse and headed out to Selman's. Warned, he grabbed a rifle and rushed over to Larn's. He arrived on top of the hill overlooking Camp Cooper just in time to see his friend led off by the posse. From here, his movements become uncertain. There are those who say he tried to round up some members of the gang and free Larn, giving up only after learning that he was dead. That sounds like something Selman would have done, had it been at all possible. But it was not possible. Things were happening too fast. Selman had tried to help and had been too late. If he were to survive at all, he now would have to escape, having seen Larn with the posse.

He made his way down the Clear Fork to Tom Lanier's Ranch in Stephens County, where he allowed himself to be seen. Then he quietly doubled back to Larn's,

---

[47]Newton Josephus Jones to J.R. Webb; Holden, *Lambshead*, p. 152.
[48]Webb, "Henry Herron."

where he took the latter's $300 chestnut sorrel stallion and rode northwest.[49]

Meanwhile, Cruger sent word for the remaining Rangers to meet the posse at Treadwell's Ranch "as soon as God would let us come," according to Newt Jones. Upon arrival, they found a meeting of the Shackelford County Vigilance Committee in progress. The implications of the arrest had begun to sink in, and the Vigilantes were "falling out among themselves" over what to do with Larn.

Sergeant Van Riper went in and talked with Cruger, who told him to take his men and follow Selman and Gross. "Van Riper told him he would not send a man after them, for he felt hurt as they had not called for our assistance in regard to Larn. Of course, they didn't want any law. They were just talking low in their hands—they too wanted the Rangers as far away that night, so they could do as they wanted with Larn."[50]

Van Riper went back to Camp Sibley, while Jones and Ranger Jack Smith rode over to see Edna Selman. "Mrs. Selman told us they would kill Larn that night. We were shocked, we hadn't thought they would go that far even though they were falling out among themselves. Mrs. Selman also said he [Larn] would have surrendered to the Rangers. She also told us that her husband, John, and his brother, Tom Selman, and John Gross had left together."[51]

Back in Albany, it was getting late, and Rye was denying lawyer Wray's efforts to get Larn released on bond. He said he would not grant bail without a pre-

---

[49]P.W. Reynolds to J.R. Webb.
[50]Newton Josephus Jones to J.R. Webb.
[51]Ibid.

liminary hearing, and it was too late in the evening to convene one.

"But, Your Honor," Wray protested, "we will place $1,200 in gold in your hands if you will give us the privilege of guarding him at the hotel over night."

"Do you understand what that proposition means, Wray?" Rye demanded.

"It only means, Your Honor, that we guarantee his presence in court tomorrow."

"No, I'm sorry to say, Wray, that your proposition spells bribery. And if it were not that the peculiar situation restrains me from giving forcible demonstration of my feelings, I would make it a personal matter with you."

When Wray said he feared the Vigilance Committee would come for Larn during the night, Rye countered with his own fears of an attempt by Selman to free him. "I do not propose to interfere with Sheriff Cruger's arrangements to hold the prisoner. I understand that he has already doubled the guards, and holds ten men in reserve."

"Well, Your Honor," Wray said in frustration, "if Larn is killed during the night, I will not be responsible for it. I have tried to do my duty."

"No one can censure you for being true to your client, Wray. And I am also conscious of performing my duty as a state officer."[52]

Years later, Rye learned that a member of the Vigilance Committee had been listening to the whole conversation through a crack in the wall. Had he granted bail, he would have met the same fate as Larn.

On hot summer evenings, people in Albany would stroll along the dusty street and visit each other. Not

---

[52]Rye, pp. 109-110.

this evening. Judge Clarke came home, told his family to get inside the house, close the shutters and stay inside until morning.

In the jail, Cruger and a deputy ran a chain through the leg irons of the twelve prisoners and locked it to a staple in the wall. The men would lie down with their feet chained together for the night. Across the road in the Shields House, Mary Larn kept watch from her second floor window. Outside of town, a group of men met, donned dustcoats, mounted up and headed for Albany. At the edge of town, they covered their faces with bandannas and approached the jail from behind, where they would not be seen by the careful Mary.[53]

Bill Cruger had posted four guards. Two of them, John Poe and Henry Cruger, were on watch. Poe sat in the doorway, with Henry Cruger in a chair behind him. The others, Ed Merritt and Robert Slack, were asleep, with their pistols under their pillows. Larn was bedded down in the southeast corner of the room. Sometime between 1 and 2 a.m., the dogs began barking. Poe heard the sound of feet. He stood up and looked out to see about thirty-five armed men with masks. He drew his pistol and told them to halt. They grabbed him, jerked him outside and took his gun. Then Henry Cruger was disarmed.

Merritt woke up to see two or three men standing over him with pistols pointed at him. He started to reach under his head for his gun but was made to lie quietly back. The noise woke Slack, who found four men with their guns cocked and pointed at him. One of them ordered him to hand over his gun. Slack was not as complacent as the others, and had to be told several

---

[53]Rye, p. 110; Interview with Joan Farmer.

times. Finally, he raised his pillow and one of the masked men took his gun.

About ten or fifteen members of the mob, as many as the jail would hold, had crowded inside. Seven or eight were strung out across the room, facing toward Larn. The rest covered the guards. No one seems to have spoken, other than the few brief words necessary to disarm the guards. Larn said nothing. Suddenly, someone started shooting and the others emptied their guns as well. Merritt estimated twenty shots were fired in all.[54]

In her room, Mary screamed. The Clarke family heard the shots and the scream, and knew what had happened. Mary, 23 years old and a widow, rushed out of the hotel and over to the jail. She got there in time to see Larn's body carried out, wrapped in a blanket, and placed on the jail's mess table.

Later that morning, Rye convened a coroner's jury, which ruled "that the deceased Jno. M. Larn came to his death by nine (9) pistol shots through the body on the morning of the 24th inst. said shots were fired by unknown parties in the Guard house in the Town of Albany, Shackelford County, Texas." Examination of the body also revealed an earlier gunshot wound through his arm that was starting to heal.[55] Mary secured a coffin in Fort Griffin. Then she and her parents took the body to the ranch and buried it close to their baby's grave.

The next issue of the Jacksboro *Frontier Echo* carried the story.

> John M. Larn, former Sheriff of Shackelford county, was arrested last week and put in the Albany jail. At night a

---

[54]Larn Docket.

[55]Larn Docket; Rye, p. 113; Holden, *Lambshead*, p. 154; Interview with Joan Farmer; Galveston *News*, July 13, 1878.

party of armed men went to the jail and shot Larn to death. Of the charges against the man we are unable to learn anything definite. About the same time an unknown man was found hanging near Griffin. Now comes a report that our former town Marshal, William C. Gilson, is missing. It is rumored that Big Bill knows considerable amount about the doings of the "Tin-Hat Brigade" and some of the members were afraid Bill had or would blow on them.[56]

In fact, Gilson had taken refuge with the Rangers. He had been a member of the group that killed Larn, although not a particularly enthusiastic one. Now he was having second thoughts about the whole thing. The Rangers took him to Fort Belknap, where he would be reasonably safe.[57]

---

[56]Jacksboro *Frontier Echo*, July 5, 1878. In his research of the Adjutant General's files in Austin in 1944, Sonnichsen ran across a list of "principal men in the Shackleford [sic] Co. Mob," which he transmitted to J.R. Webb. Listed are W.R. Cruger, sheriff; James Diaper [i.e., Draper], deputy sheriff; W.H. Ledbetter, county judge; G.R. Carter, J.H. and A. (?), Samuel Connor, John Poe, John Jacobs, W.C. Gilson, C.K. Stribling, John Jackson and George Mathews. At the time, Sonnichsen speculated this list was given by John Selman, and said, "I doubt if it can be trusted, and it isn't a very good thing to have lying around . . ." However, it is generally accepted as containing many of the men involved in the death of John Larn. In my own correspondence with Sonnichsen, during the winter of 1986-87, he expressed a belief that at least some of Larn's in-laws were involved, a belief which is widespread and which I share. In addition, Bill Howsley admitted to Phin Reynolds that he was among those who killed Larn and "left the impression" that the leader of the group was one of Phin's own brothers. (P.W. Reynolds to J.R. Webb, 1945).

[57]Newton Josephus Jones to J.R. Webb.

8

The Aftermath

The Rangers began investigating the Larn killing almost immediately. A few days later, Newt Jones ran into John William Poe, who in addition to his duties as Vigilante and none-too-careful jail guard, also served as town marshal of Fort Griffin. Jones didn't trust Poe, and as they talked, he kept his finger on his Winchester, just in case. The upshot of the conversation was that the Rangers intended to stop the killings and were gathering evidence against the committee. "Poe said not a word, but looked at me," Jones said.

About the same time, the posse which had gone after Selman, about a dozen men in all, returned empty handed. Jones recognized Glen Reynolds in the group and walked up to him.

"Glen, I want to have a private talk with you," he said.

Once they were out of earshot, Jones leveled with him. "We cannot understand the situation. We have been told that they would kill us just the same as they would Larn."

Reynolds replied, "If you are going to get evidence, there is nothing they would not do to stop it. I was about thirty miles from here, but they sent for me to come down, but I shouldn't have come, and I never expect to be with them again."

Jones and Jack Smith were also offered a substantial bribe by a member of the Vigilance Committee, to ease off on the investigation. "But Smith started cursing him and told him we did not want that kind of money and did not let him get any further."

The situation was dangerous. When Major Jones asked Sergeant Van Riper for details of the Larn case and any other incidents in the area, he took two Rangers and Gilson to Austin to report in person, since he "did not think best to communicate with Austin by telegraph." Newt Jones, Smith and another Ranger remained in camp near Fort Belknap, checking with the telegraph office in Graham each day to see if Van Riper had any orders for them. After ten days, they returned to Camp Sibley, two miles north of Fort Griffin, where two men were kept on guard all the time, "as we did not know whether we would be attacked or not." Each day they checked the telegraph office in Griffin. Finally, they were ordered to Denton, where they were to join Captain June Peak's company in pursuit of Sam Bass. Captain G.W. Arrington was ordered back to Fort Griffin.[1]

In his orders to Arrington, Major Jones told him to "be particularly careful to avoid, and *guard your men against* [Jones' emphasis] any undue sympathy with or prejudice against any of the parties to the feud which exists in that section.[2]

Obviously the Shackelford strings were still being pulled in Austin. The Rangers who had lived through

[1]Newton Josephus Jones to J.R. Webb; John B. Jones to Van Riper, July 6, 1878, in Letters.

the Larn affair had very strong opinions, few sympathies, and were not particularly interested in whom they offended.

Selman was still on the loose. After riding off on Larn's horse, he led the posse to the foot of the plains. There, the Shackelford County men found the horse where Selman had abandoned it and lost his trail. Not long afterward, Edna Selman died in premature childbirth. The Selman children were turned over to J.C. McGrew, whose wife was Mrs. Selman's niece.[3]

On September 10, 1880, the Shackelford County grand jury indicted John Selman on ten counts of cattle theft. The list of charges takes five pages in the district court docket.[4] By then, Selman was in jail in Fort Davis in West Texas for a series of gangster activities there. The Rangers investigating the situation were more interested in returning him to Shackelford County than in building a case in Fort Davis. But Bill Cruger wasn't particularly interested in getting him back. He wanted the whole Larn affair behind him, and wasn't sure he could guarantee Selman's safety. Initially he was sent to Comanche, and from there, was returned to Albany. Cruger placed him under the guard of Bill Jeffries, Bill Howsley and George Shields, who took him to Fort Griffin. Behind Conrad's store, he was given "a flea bitten horse belonging to John Sauers." His guards shook hands with him and told him to ride. Some shots were fired into the air for effect, and John Selman was out of their lives, a free man. Sauer's employer, George

[2]Jones to Arrington, July 13, 1878, in Letters.

[3]Robert Nail to Leon C. Metz, ND, Nail Papers; Metz to Nail, Jan. 14, 1964, Nail Papers; Metz, *John Selman*, pp. 93-94.

[4]Shackelford County, Minutes of the District Court, Vol. A, 6-7-[18]75 to 3-1-[18]84, pp. 258-262.

Reynolds, provided another horse to replace the one Selman had used in his "escape."[5]

On January 11, 1881, alias capias warrants were issued for Selman. It was all a formality. In May, the grand jury dismissed all cases against him "for reasons that there is not sufficient evidence to be obtained to secure a conviction."[6]

Selman lived almost eighteen years after the Larn affair. Following a checkered career on both sides of the law, he settled down to become a police officer in El Paso. On August 19, 1895, he killed John Wesley Hardin in the Acme Saloon. Less than a year later, Selman himself was dead. Drunk, he got into an argument with Deputy U.S. Marshal George Scarborough. Details are obscure, but guns flashed. The next day, April 6, 1896, John Selman died following surgery.

John William Poe, whose Vigilante membership may have caused him to be less than vigilant the night they came for Larn, fared better than most. He remained a lawman of sorts, and was with Pat Garrett the night he shot Billy the Kid in New Mexico. Although Poe and Garrett were buffalo hunters in Griffin about the same time, there is no indication they knew each other before teaming up to get Billy. Garrett later assisted in Poe's efforts to marry Sophie Alberding, who became his biographer and chief admirer.[8] Sophie Poe's *Buckboard Days* generally holds up as a source book of the frontier period. However, her information on the feud was provided by her husband, who embellished Larn's

[5]Metz, *John Selman*, pp. 120-123, quote from P.W. Reynolds to J.R. Webb, Webb Papers; W.R. Cruger to Major Jones, July 2, 1880, typescript in Webb Papers.

[6]Shackelford County, Minutes of the District Court, Vol. A, pp. 284-285; Nail to Metz.

[7]Metz, *John Selman*, pp. 198-200.

[8]Metz, *Pat Garrett*, p. 132; Sophie Poe, *Buckboard Days*, pp. 169-170.

death for her benefit and cast himself as a hero. As such, the early chapters come out pretty much the Gospel According to John William.

Bill Cruger resigned as sheriff in 1880 and moved to Albany, Georgia, the town which had given its name to the county seat of Shackelford County. He died there on December 29, 1882, at the age of 34.[9]

Mary Mathews Larn eventually married the Rev. John Brown, a self-righteous Scottish minister who presided over Presbyterian affairs in the area. The Rev. Mr. Brown seems to have had a few faults of his own. Judge Clarke despised him "like no other man." Brown took her east, where the marriage eventually fell apart. She wrote her father that she wanted to come home, and George Reynolds was sent to bring her back. Years later, she was heard to say, "I married a cow thief the first time, and a preacher the second, and I do believe the cow thief was the best man." Mary lived on until February 12, 1946, when she died in Los Angeles, California.[10]

Will Larn died almost 60 years later, and without marrying. The ranch at Camp Cooper came into possession of Mary's brother, J.A. (Budd) Mathews. He made the first renovation, in which Larn's cupola was removed. Budd used the house strictly as headquarters, maintaining his home elsewhere. His wife Sallie detested the place because of its associations with Larn. Eventually, it was purchased by J.C. Putnam.[11]

With the principals of the Larn affair dead, on the run, or under the scrutiny of the Rangers, the Shackel-

[9]D.C. Campbell Sr., sheriff, Dougherty County, Albany, Georgia, to J.R. Webb, July 12, 1945, Webb Papers.

[10]Miss Ollie Clarke; Bob Green to Robert Nail, citing George Newcombe; miscellaneous notes, all in Nail Papers.

[11]Bob Green to Robert Nail; Interview with Mrs. J.C. Putnam.

ford County Feud, as the Vigilance period is officially known, began winding down. The committee itself would linger on for awhile. In fact, it would look monumentally foolish through the courage and tenacity of one man, before finally playing itself out.

Even so, by August 31, 1878, just two months after Larn's death, Arrington was able to write Major Jones, "I have conversed with quite a number of the good citizens and find everything quiet and from what I can glean I am satisfied that at *one* [Arrington's emphasis] time nearly everybody belonged to the mob—but the good men are now satisfied that law and order can be maintained without lynch law, and the extremists, the smart young men *like* it, from so much experience in the business—and they want to hold on to the substantial men as backers.

"However, I think by a mild course, first gaining confidence of the masses, everything will work well."[12]

Everything did work out eventually, at least from an official point of view. But John Larn's dual personality left him many friends in Shackelford County, and they remained bitter until the end of their days. In 1934, as Ben O. Grant prepared his pioneering thesis on the county, he interviewed Uncle Joe McCombs, the buffalo hunter. That portion of the thesis deserves to be reprinted in its entirety, as a fitting end to this period in the life of the Flat:

> "I was on the buffalo range, son, when it happened, but about twenty-five or thirty men rode up to the jail and shot Larn down like he was a dog. They never give him no chance at all."
>
> Here the old man broke down and cried as if he were a baby; muttering under his breath as if to himself, he said

---

[12]Arrington to Jones, Aug. 31, 1878, in Letters.

"My God! if I had been there!" When asked if he believed that Larn was taking cattle that did not belong to him, he said:

"I guess he was, son, but it was common in them days, and I don't see why they pitched in on him. He was one of the best friends I ever had; he saved my life once and if I could, I would have done as much for him."[13]

---

[13]Grant, *Early History*, pp. 92-93.

9

The Strange Case of
James A. Brock

In John W. Thomason's novel *Lone Star Preacher*, one of Praxiteles Swan's sayings was, "If you are diligent in business, you stand before kings...you do not stand before mean men."[1] James A. Brock was diligent in business. And while he never stood before a king, he faced down something far more deadly. He defied the Shackelford County Vigilance Committee.

Brock lived in Fort Griffin during its heyday, a time when Texas was being flooded with newcomers. "Old families" were families that had been around since before the War Between the States, and the "great families" were the ones who had seen the Republic. The iron-clad clannishness that would become the hallmark of Texas families was just beginning to develop, and one relative might turn on another at the drop of a branding iron.

By all accounts, Brock would have been easy to turn against. Henry Herron said he was "a little mysterious in his manners and was not popular. He wore a stove pipe hat, dressed different from others, did not drink, and held himself aloof from others, and became known

---

[1] John W. Thomason, *Lone Star Preacher*, p. 279.

as a 'high hatter' and as being stuck up."[2] Don Biggers called him "a shrewd, far-sighted business man, who devoted most of his time to attending to Brock's business and taking advantage of every opportunity to honorably make a dollar. He wasn't much of a 'mixer' and nothing of a sport, made no grand-stand plays for popularity and with no further effort or offense on his part succeeded in getting the cold indifference of the gang around Fort Griffin, and in those days the cold indifference of the gang around a Western town was a proposition to be reckoned with should emergency require the power and pull of influential friends."[3]

Brock arrived from Indiana not long after the post was founded on Government Hill, and held a position in the post trader's store. He transacted his own business on the side and was soon able to open up his own store. By then cattle were starting to come through Fort Griffin. As the herds passed through, they left "drags," calves too young and cattle too weak to keep up. These drags were there for the taking, and Brock took. They, together with the money he had saved from his store, allowed him to build a sizeable herd of his own, and before too long, Brock was in the cattle business. He hired a black cowhand named Nick to look after them while Brock tended to his store. Eventually, the herd grew too large for one man, and Brock sent back to Indiana for his cousins, Ed and Frank Woosley. With their arrival, Brock's troubles began.[4]

According to the agreement, the Woosleys would run the ranch in return for half of the increase in the herd. For a while, things went well. The herd built up

[2]Henry Herron to J.R. Webb.
[3]Biggers, pp. 46-47.
[4]Sallie Reynolds Mathews, *Interwoven*, p. 136; Biggers, p. 46; Grant, p. 90.

and Brock made money. No one much cared for Frank Woosley, either, but he was a shade more popular than Brock.[5]

The ranching operation reached the point where Brock felt it best to close out the store and give his full attention to cattle. When time came to settle with Frank Woosley, the latter refused the one-half increase and demanded more. Apparently Brock turned him down, because the matter ended up in court.[6]

The hearing was held on October 20, 1877, on Cause No. 25, Frank Woosley vs. James A. Brock, motion for Sequestration. The dispute centered on cattle, horses and mules from a herd owned by Brock and one John F. Brown, a portion of which were branded WOO. The court awarded the stock thus branded and its increase to Woosley. However, it also awarded compensation of $900 and costs to Brock. The majority of the judgment was stayed three months to allow each side time to satisfy its obligations.[7]

That should have ended the whole thing, but it didn't. Brock and Frank Woosley continued to quarrel. Words were exchanged within earshot of others, and one witness may have been a member of the Vigilance Committee. A few days later Woosley rode up to California Ranch, where Budd and Sallie Mathews lived. He was looking for the Mathews cow outfit, and Sallie gave him directions to where she thought it might be. As she later remembered, "He got down off his horse, adjusted his saddle, mounted again and rode away. That was the last ever seen of him in West Texas."[8]

---

[5]Grant, p. 90; Herron to Webb.
[6]Grant, p. 90; Shackelford County, Minutes of the District Court, Vol. A, p. 104.
[7]Shackelford County, Minutes of the District Court, Vol. A, p. 104.
[8]Grant, p. 90; Sallie Reynolds Mathews, *Interwoven*, p. 136.

Woosley had taken some extra saddle horses with him. They were found the following day. Bill Cruger began an official investigation while the Vigilance Committee began an unofficial one. A key piece of evidence was missing, however, and that was Woosley's body. Still, Cruger arrested Brock on charges of cattle theft, to keep him on ice in the Albany jail until the investigation was completed.[9]

The Vigilantes seemed unsure of what to do. Most were convinced Brock was guilty, but some members did not want to act until a body was found. Discussing the case with Ben Grant in 1935, A.S. Swan remembered being on guard in the jail about midnight, the time when the Vigilantes generally rode. Sure enough, he heard hoofbeats. He slipped into the jail, unfastened the chains which held Brock to the floor, and gave him a gun. Then they locked themselves inside, both armed, and waited.

"They rode up within fifty yards of the jail and stopped; we could hear them talking but could not understand what they said. They talked for ten minutes or more and some of them sounded like they were mad about something from their voices. After they had talked for a while they rode away. Brock and I both came out of the jail and listened to them leave. Brock still had my gun and handed it to me as soon as the horses had gone out of hearing." Swan admitted to being scared, but said Brock was calm through it all.[10]

The following morning, Brock asked Cruger for permission to go into Fort Griffin. Cruger agreed and said he would send Special Deputy Shields along with him. Brock would have none of that, since Shields was

[9]Henry Herron to J.R. Webb; Biggers, p. 47.
[10]Grant, p. 91.

"sympathetic to the Vigilantes." Instead he asked that John Meyer Herron, Henry's father, go with him. Cruger agreed and Brock rode up to Griffin with Shields and John Herron. There, he disposed of his cattle holdings and now had enough money for bond.

Although it was night by the time Brock's business affairs were settled, Shields wanted to return to Albany immediately. On the other hand, Brock wanted to wait until daylight. John Herron backed him. He wasn't about to have his prisoner strung up by night riders. The three returned to Albany the following day and Brock was released on bond.[11]

The Vigilance Committee wasn't through yet. About three days later, they hauled out Nick, Brock's black hired hand, and strung him up. Just before he strangled, they cut him down and tried to force him to tell what Brock did with Woosley. Nick refused. Three times, he was strung up and cut down just before dying. Each time, he refused to talk. Finally, the committee was convinced that he knew nothing, and turned him loose.[12]

Brock himself was neither impressed nor intimidated by a bunch of Vigilantes. He confronted several people whom he suspected of being members of the committee, and put them on notice that if he left town, he would tell them where he was heading and when he planned to be back. The man's determination to stay in town and prove his innocence was becoming very embarrassing.

Henry Herron was buttonholed by a man whom he suspected of being the leader of the committee. The man told him Woosley's bones had reportedly been

---

[11]Herron to J.R. Webb.
[12]Biggers, p. 47; Herron to J.R. Webb.

found in Throckmorton County and insisted that Herron, as a deputy, should do something about it.

"I replied that if Woosley's body was found, the grand jury could indict him. But he replied that they were not positive. I did not believe the report about the finding of Woosley's bones, so I told him that I was of the opinion that Brock was innocent and if anything happened to him, I was going to Austin and tell the authorities there all that I knew."[13]

Herron was sure the Vigilantes would try something that night, and he hunted up Brock and told him so. When Brock did not appear concerned, Herron decided to stay with him that night. After supper they went to an upstairs room in a building belonging to John Herron, about where the Albany post office now stands. They had a shotgun, a Winchester rifle and Henry's pistol. The room was entered from an outside stairway, and the door was barricaded with a heavy timber. Sitting in the room, they went over the case again. Brock appeared unsure as to what had actually happened, but was positive Woosley was still alive and said he intended to find him. About 10 p.m., Brock fell into a sound sleep which continued until the next morning. Herron was unable to sleep at all, and when the night was over, told Brock he was on his own.[14]

Although the grand jury returned several indictments against Brock on minor offenses, it refused to consider murder, on the grounds that there was no evidence Woosley was actually dead. Brock then announced that he intended to find the man alive and prove his innocence. He gave notice that he would leave the area, but he would always be in contact with

[13]Herron to J.R. Webb.
[14]Ibid.

someone there, keeping them posted of his whereabouts and plans. Then he deposited $1,000 in the
bank as a reward for anyone who could either produce
Woosley alive or provide information which would
clear up the case. He ordered post cards with Woosley's
picture and the reward offer, which he sent throughout
the United States, Canada and Mexico. Finally he left
on his own search, which would take the next fourteen
years. During the entire time, he always notified someone in Shackelford County of his whereabouts.

Henry Herron saw Brock a year later in El Paso. The
two went over to Juarez, where Brock could talk of
nothing but the case. "Finally," Herron said, "I told him
that he just talked so much about it that sometimes I
thought he was guilty. He seemed deeply hurt and told
me that he was sorry I felt that way about it, but that it
meant everything to him to clear his name."[15]

Brock traveled on his search until his money ran out.
Then he worked at odd jobs, saving enough money to
resume his search. When that money gave out, he
would work again until he had saved some more.

More than a decade after Woosley's disappearance,
two of Brock's old acquaintances were sitting in a
restaurant in Las Vegas, New Mexico, "when a rather
striking individual walked in. He was dressed in a
leather shirt and buckskin pants, and his long beard
and general appearance indicated that he had just returned probably from a long prospecting tour in the
mountains. Noticing us, the man walked directly to
where we were, called us by name and extended his
hand. Then we recognized him. It was Brock..."

Brock refused an invitation for lunch, but did sit
with the pair. He recounted walking "from ranch to

---

[15]Biggers, p. 48; Herron to J.R. Webb.

ranch in the mountains along the Rio Grande, how he had trudged from mining camp to mining camp in the West, how he had almost perished from cold and hunger along the Canadian border, and had gone from town to town hunting the man with whose death he stood charged. He showed us his hands, once as white and tender as a woman's but now rough, chapped and corn-covered, and told us how he had worked at everything from driving freight wagons to slinging a pick in the mines, only to put his scanty earnings into the search for the missing man."

After lunch, the two accompanied Brock to his room, where they talked for three hours. Brock's account of his search fascinated them. "Here was a place where some detective had located a man in every particular corresponding to the missing man, and to this place Brock had gone full of hope, only to be disappointed. Here he had met with some cruel, pleasant or unusual experience. To me it was the most remarkable experience of which I had ever known, the most wonderful story to which I had ever listened."

As his two friends got ready to leave, Brock remarked, "If I live another year and keep sufficiently well to work and travel, I will find that man. Just now I have got to work awhile, as I must have $24 to defray some necessary expenses, but fortunately, I am able to work and know where I can get a very good job."

One of the men reached into his wallet and took out the twenty-four dollars. Brock's lip quivered and his eyes filled with tears, but he shook his head. He had stood on his own throughout the search, and would stand on his own now.[16]

It was now into the 1890s. The Shackelford County

---

[16]Biggers, p. 49-50.

Vigilance Committee, having been torn asunder by Larn and Selman, had long since vanished into history. Fort Griffin itself was largely abandoned and crumbling into ruins. Still, Brock's quest continued. Then, almost a year to the day after meeting his friends in Las Vegas, the telegraph wires flashed the news. A quiet, unassuming resident of Arkansas had positively been identified as Frank Woosley.

A Tennessee law enforcement officer had gone to Arkansas to look for a man wanted in his state. He had one of Brock's old reward cards, and saw a man he thought resembled the picture. A telegram was sent to Brock, who rushed down to Arkansas. Meanwhile, the Tennessee officer found out where Woosley lived, and everything else he could about him.

Brock arrived and agreed the man was Woosley, even though he was living under an assumed name. He was bundled off to Indiana, where relatives confirmed his identity and provided affidavits. Now that it was all out in the open, Woosley told a story about having been in an accident on the range and losing his memory. He wandered for days before he recovered enough to strike out for civilization. Eventually he arrived in Arkansas, where he had married, settled down and was raising a family when he was discovered.

No one in Shackelford County believed it, particularly since he had been subscribing to the Albany paper in his step-son's name during his stay in Arkansas. In Albany, it was commonly thought that Frank and Ed Woosley had decided to fabricate Frank's disapperance and possible murder, in hopes the Vigilantes would make short work of Brock. With him out of the way, Frank would reappear with some sort of convincing story and the two would claim the estate. They reckoned without two things—that some of the Vigilantes would demand more proof than a simple disappearance, and that Brock himself would devote so much of his life to proving his innocence.

James A. Brock returned to Albany and cleared his name. Ed Woosley, who had been in ill health, had long since died and Frank disappeared into obscurity.[17]

Sallie Reynolds Mathews summed up the Brock case in a single phrase. She said, "it wrecked the life of an innocent man."[18] Maybe. But Brock didn't necessarily think so. As Henry Herron observed, "He had spent 14 years and also all of his money and many sleepless nights and days of worry in clearing his name, but it was worth it all to him. He was that kind of man."[19]

---

[17]Biggers, p. 50; Herron to J.R. Webb.
[18]Mathews, *Interwoven*, p. 138.
[19]Herron to J.R. Webb.

10

The Downtown
Merchants

Up until now, it might seem that life in the Flat consisted primarily of lynchings and shootings, and that the only businesses in town were hunting outfitters, saloons and sporting palaces. There was a disproportionate number of these, to be sure. But someone had to provide goods and services to the outfitters, saloonkeepers and soiled doves. There had to be druggists, dry goods vendors, ironmongers and barbers. As more people moved into the area, the demand for the amenities of civilization increased, creating a market for such things as stationery and Christmas toys. Finally, there was that hallmark of mercantile respectability, the newspaper.

Fort Griffin was, in fact, the mercantile center of the Texas frontier. Jacksboro had done all right as a cowtown for awhile, but it had seen its day. Now it supported itself with the county seat, a stagecoach stop and with the military at Fort Richardson, but was too far removed from the major trails to retain the importance it once had. The trails were continually moving westward, and that meant everything on the frontier. The military trails, buffalo trails and cattle trails determined whether a town grew, and Fort Griffin was in the middle of them all. The Flat's leading merchant, Frank Conrad, could rightfully claim his emporium as the largest between Fort Worth and El Paso.

Conrad got his start, as did the business community as a whole, with the post trade at Fort Griffin proper. The first post trader had been a man named Hicks. The business passed through another owner or two, until Conrad arrived from Fort McKavett and took over the contract about 1870.[1]

Unlike the modern military post exchange, the frontier post trader's was open to anyone. In fact, most of the business seems to have been civilian, rather than military, and for a long time the trader appears to have been the only real source of goods and services in the area. Then Sam Newcomb built a store down in the Flat, and a business community started to grow. These early stores were built haphazardly. Typical of the frontier, they were part tent, part shack, with no idea of being permanent. No one had surveyed the town, or had even intended for a town to be there. It just happened. Buildings went up on any convenient spot, and if they were out of line with everyone else, that was all right.[2]

The early businesses were geared toward two principle clients, buffalo hunters and soldiers. Virtually everyone was a hunt outfitter of some sort, and virtually everyone had a saloon attached to his store.[3] But soldiers and hide hunters also needed transportation, and this involved horses and mules. To answer the demand, Pete Haverty kept a livery stable, and did a

---

[1]John Chadbourne Irwin to J.R. Webb.
[2]P.W. Reynolds to J.R. Webb; Grant, p. 71.
[3]Grant, p. 71.

little horse and mule racing on th side. He was proud of his racing stock, and the Fort Griffin *Echo* noted:

> Pete Haverty brags on having the fastest trotting horse and the fastest running mule in the county and is ready to back either at any time. He also knows a man and will back him as a runner against any other man in the State.[4]

Henry Herron remembered Haverty's horse as a paint "which could outrun anything in the country. He had a reputation far and wide on the frontier, and an unbeaten record for several years. Finally a fellow came along driving a grizzled grey [hitched] to a buggy. The calves had chewed off the old horse's mane and tail, or so it appeared, and I think it was intended that he should look that way. He matched a race with Haverty and also took a number of side bets. He beat Haverty's horse to a frazzle, cleaned Haverty out of $500, and ruined the reputation of his paint horse."[15]

Another businessman involved in transportation was Hank Smith. Smith was originally from one of the minor German states. Orphaned at age 12, he immigrated to the U.S. to live with his sister. He knocked around the mining camps of Arizona and New Mexico, and served for a time in a frontier detachment during the War Between the States. When the war ended, he divided his time between Fort Quitman and El Paso, with various mercantile and freight enterprises. However, he seems to have had problems with creditors in El Paso, and the year 1871 found him in Fort Griffin, where he bought two lots. The following year, he received the hay contract for the post and expanded into the freight business.[6]

---

[4]Fort Griffin *Echo*, Jan. 4, 1879.   [5]J.R. Webb, "Henry Herron."
[6]Mrs. H.C. Smith to Mody Boatwright, Apr. 22, 1921, miscellaneous files, Hank Smith Papers.

In 1874, Smith was also clerking in the post trader's at Fort Griffin, when he married Elizabeth Boyle, recently emigrated from Scotland. By this time, he was firmly established in the area, and his bride recalled the "many nice presents of Silver and Linen and other things." Among the wedding guests were Colonel Buell, post commander, and the officers.[7]

The Smiths soon opened a store of their own in Fort Griffin. The mercantile community they joined seems to have had some sort of gentleman's agreement over wages and prices. While this kept the merchants from ruining each other, it operated to the detriment of those who depended on them for a living. A disgruntled wage-earner named Bob MacGregor looked back on the early days of the Flat and wrote:

> Dear to the memory of some will be the palmy days of Hicks the post trader. to illustrate the Case
>
> There is Brock with his Rancho of improved Stock. his hired men are well paid and well fed.
>
> The Sallon to illustrate it I will simply state that one half the proceeds are Smiths and the other half George Wilhelms and the poor small half to Hicks.
>
> Smith's brothers by marriage the Boyles are enabled to take Contracts Cheaper than anybody else.
>
> George Wilhelm (Inocence personified) Keeps from 6 to 10 men employed year around. he takes Contracts Cheaper than anybody and Colects revenue enough in the bar room, to pay and feed them better than any man in Shackleford County. I wood not object were it not that I am a working man with a large family to support and I want a fair price for my labor.[8]

The complaint found its way to Smith, who filed it with his other papers.

---

[7]Mrs. H.C. Smith to Miss Mattie Anderson, Hank Smith Papers.
[8]Hank Smith Papers.

Success in business did not free the Smiths from the lawlessness which permeated the Flat. One time, Smith was due in court in Albany, and decided to make a family trip of it. He took his wife and children, leaving the store in the care of Henry Jacobs, who was working there as a clerk. Jacobs moved his wife and two children into Mrs. Smith's upstairs room, so the building would be occupied at all times during the family's absence.

On Saturday, the day the Smiths left, nine men came into the store. Claiming to be Rangers, they looked it over and departed. The following day, they were back, guns in hands, to clean the place out. Smith kept a large stock of buffalo guns and ammunition, and Jacobs and a man named Hawes were ready to make a fight of it. The frightened Mrs. Jacobs dissuaded them. The outlaws took everything, including Mrs. Smith's supply of medicines, four horses and Hawes' watch. They even went so far as to make Jacobs pull off his boots and hand them over.[9]

The robbery notwithstanding, the Smiths did well. When Henry Herron first arrived in Fort Griffin, the only hotel in town was Planter's. It was a two-story building opposite Pete Haverty's livery stable, and was run by Jack Schwartz.[10] Then the Smiths expanded into the hotel business, opening the Occidental. They weren't in it for long. Hank Smith had backed Charles Tasker of Fort Griffin in a ranch at Blanco Canyon. Tasker, known locally as Lord Tasker for his high and mighty ways, wasn't able to make a go of it, and in 1876, Smith took the ranch over for debt. Two years later, he moved his family there and got out of the hotel business. Another hotel, the Southern, operated

[9]Mrs. H.C. Smith to Miss Alma Burke, Mrs. H.C. Smith to Miss Mattie Anderson, Hank Smith Papers.   [10]J.R. Webb, "Henry Herron."

for awhile, but by late 1878, Frank Conrad and Charley Rath were ready to move their emporium down from Government Hill and into town. They took over the Southern and refitted it for a warehouse and a post office, leaving Planter's once again with the boast that it was "The only hotel in town and the best one on the frontier."[11]

The Fort Griffin *Echo*'s assessment of Planter's, possibly influenced by regular advertising, was that Schwartz "dispenses hospitality to all transients, and his agreeable lady has already established a reputation second to none as a hostess."[12] Schwartz ordered his tea directly from Japan, and once claimed to have a dispatch "stating that his cargo of tea was raised in the Imperial garden and only sold because of the immense crop."[13]

Schwartz's cargo of imperial tea didn't threaten the saloons. Hunter's Retreat was a popular watering hole, as was Charley Meyers'. But the saloons had competition from the more respectable segment of the community. In its very first issue from Fort Griffin, on January 4, 1879, the *Echo* announced:

> H.L. Seward, deputy U.S. Marshal, visited the town this week and carried off our druggist, Dr. Lignoski, on charges of violations of the revenue law. We are inclined to think the case is one of many where the accused has not complied strictly with the letter of the law, yet intentionally has not violated it.[14]

Apparently the court in Fort Worth agreed, because Dr. Lignoski returned to Fort Griffin a few days later.

[11]Ibid.; Mrs. H.C. Smith to Miss Alma Burke; Fort Griffin *Echo*, Jan. 4, 1879; quote from *Echo*, June 14, 1879.

[12]Fort Griffin *Echo*, Jan. 4, 1879.

[13]Ibid., Feb. 2, 1881.

[14]Ibid., Jan. 4, 1879.

The case had been dismissed.[15] Given these circumstances, it is hard to resist a snicker at an announcement which later appeared in the *Echo*'s "personals" column:

> The best whisky in Shackelford county is to be found at Dr. Lignoski's drug stor [sic] in this place. Sold for medicinal purposes.

Farther down that same page, the doc gave notice he was turning his unpaid accounts over for collection.[16]

The Flat was booming. Along about 1876, it occurred to many people that Fort Griffin might become permanent after all. The layout of the town began to take on some semblance of order, with the business district fronting on Griffin Avenue. More substantial buildings were raised.[17] Currency was scarce and most people paid by check. That didn't bother Frank Conrad, who was the town's unofficial banker. Conrad had his rivals, chief among whom was F.B. York, who originally came from Fort Dodge, Kansas. York had a warehouse which was "a large and commodious building, and well filled. In his yard, wagons enough are packed to move the baggage of an entire regiment." Among other things, York alleviated the currency shortage by putting in a bank and jobbing house.[18]

Some of the other leading merchants were E. Frankel, who operated a saloon and emporium, and Hunter, Evans Co., Dry Goods. J.M. Cupp & Bro. Hardware Store was described as "a favorite resort for buffalo hunters; where everything can be had, or if it is not on hand the article can be made from the making of horse

---

[15]Ibid., Jan. 11, 1879.

[16]Ibid., June 14, 1879.

[17]Grant, p. 72.

[18]Fort Griffin *Echo*, Jan. 4, 1879; Fort Worth *Democrat*, Apr. 15, 1878.

shoes to the mending of a looking glass."[19] For awhile, there was a Jewish businessman named Marks, whom locals called "Cheap John." Marks was murdered in Haskel County in 1879. A Fort Worth gambler named Frank Schmidt was tried for it, but was acquitted.[20]

All things considered, it was a glorious time for the Flat, a time in which "commercialism was the dominant power that ruled."[21] Recalling his first sight of the town, Edgar Rye wrote:

> "The one long street, from the foot of the hill through the town to the crossing of the Clear Fork, was alive with men and horses and in many places near the supply stores wagons were jammed together in a way that almost stopped travel...
>
> It was the palmy days of Fort Griffin, when money flowed like water through the avenues of businesses, and men handled it with the same careless indifference that merchants handled bacon, flour and potatoes. Not hundreds but thousands of dollars changed hands each day. And one day spent in the Flat, and one night among the denizens who frequented the resorts, would convince any man that it was not a question of price, but whether the supply would hold out.[22]

Presiding benignly over it all, first from his perch on Government Hill, and then from his vast warehouses in the Flat, was Frank Conrad. On one particular day he did $4,000 worth of business, of which $2,500 was for guns and ammunition.[23] Anything Conrad had was for sale, including the building. In July 1879, his two-story building was moved to Throckmorton County, where he had sold it to serve as the courthouse.[24]

---

[19]Fort Griffin *Echo*, Jan. 4, 1879.

[20]J.R. Webb, "Henry Herron."

[21]Rye, p. 27.

[22]Ibid., pp. 27, 29.

[23]C.C. Rister, "The Significance of the Destruction of the Buffalo in the Southwest," in *SWHQ*, July 1929, p. 46.

[24]Fort Griffin *Echo*, July 19, 1879.

He had a series of partners in his early years, finally settling on Charley Rath, the ex-buffalo hunter and hide merchant from Kansas. After Rath withdrew in 1879, Conrad went on alone, operating as F.E. Conrad and Co. Either way, he offered the "Largest & most Complete Stock West of Fort Worth."[26]

If there was a way to make money, Conrad had a hand in it. When his wagons carried hides to Fort Worth, they returned with cargoes of corn for horse fodder. This brought some complaints from the Rangers assigned to police the area, who felt he charged extra when they were buying. In one report to Austin, Lieutenant G.W. Campbell pointed out that while Conrad and Rath "can furnish corn as cheap as any one can," it ranged from $1.25 to $1.40 a bushel, which he considered too high. "[I] do not know why Msrs Conrad and Rath charge me more than they do the Buffalo hunters," he wrote. Still, the state fared better than the Army, since he also noted that they had sold a thousand bushels to Colonel Mackenzie for the Fourth Cavalry at $2 a bushel.[26]

In addition to his other interests, Conrad was the Flat's postmaster. He also served as agent for the stage line, which was the only public transportation in and out of Fort Griffin. Not that it was any easy way to make money. Local companies did not always share the Butterfield Overland's obsession with schedules and service. And when the local stage line cut back or discontinued service, it cut into the agent's income. Stage lines weren't always sure of what they wanted to do. In March 1876, the El Paso Stage Company discontinued the Fort Griffin mail route and sent its stock to Fort Concho. A rider was hired to carry the

[25]Ibid., June 17, 1879.
[26]G. W. Campbell to Major John Jones, Jan. 31, 1878, in "Letters."

mail from the Flat to Jacksboro.[27] Yet only a month later, the stage line resumed service to Fort Griffin.[28] Since no explanation was ever offered for the cut or resumption of service, we must assume that people on the frontier were used to it.

Much of the information on daily life at Fort Griffin comes from newspapers of the period. They are often discounted as primary sources, when in fact, they probably reflect the community as closely as anything. They provide the small details of the day-to-day activities, sometimes neglected or taken for granted in letters, diaries and memoirs. Because of their dependence on advertising, they are often the best source of information on the business community. Fort Griffin was covered thoroughly, first by the Jacksboro *Frontier Echo* and then the Fort Griffin *Echo*. The two papers were actually one and the same, and both were the product of G.W. Robson. Little is known about his early career, which is a shame, since he was one of the most honest, influential and highly respected editors of the frontier.[29] He appears to have been a railroad engineer in Kansas, but there is no information beyond that. The tone of his articles, plus his declining health during his years of publication in Jacksboro would place him about late middle age.

Robson, who was almost universally called "Captain," showed up in Jacksboro in 1875, and established the *Frontier Echo*. Once in business, he set about stamping the area with his own brand of frontier journalism. He championed the cattlemen, since for all practical purposes, they were the local economy. His personals

---

[27]Jacksboro *Frontier Echo*, March 21, 1876.

[28]Ibid., Apr. 28, 1878.

[29]Elsa Turner, Albany, TX, to Charles M. Robinson III; W.C. Holden, "Frontier Journalism in West Texas," *SWHQ*, Jan. 1929, p. 214.

column detailed the comings and goings and the various doings of his friends and associates. Dan Brown's store was his biggest advertiser, and he played Brown up with the same unabashed enthusiasm he would later give to Frank Conrad in Fort Griffin. He was a strong advocate of law and order; Vernon's if possible and Lynch's if necessary. He took a knight-errant's interest in the ladies of the community, and wrote up each wedding as if he were the father of the bride.[30]

Ironically, Robson arrived in Jacksboro about the time it was going into decline, and Fort Griffin was taking over as the economic center. Over the next three years, more and more of his news came from the Flat until, in December 1878, he published his last issue of the *Frontier Echo*. He was moving to Fort Griffin.

It took Robson only a few days to settle in at the Flat. He already knew many of the leading citizens, and on January 4, 1879, Volume 1, Number 1 of the Fort Griffin *Echo* hit the streets. In it, he wrote;

> Having had some experience of publishing a newspaper on the frontier, we flatter ourselves that we know a little regarding the wants of a frontier community and will ever be found ready to assist the people so far as we are able.[31]

Robson was more than able. He came into his own in the Flat. He went fishing with the "boys" along the Clear Fork. He went to picnics and attended all the civic functions. He even covered the anti-saloon league, although he balanced it with such personals as, "Johnny Hammond can draw a schooner of iced beer with more grace and less foam than any man in the village."[32] Robson may not have been an expert on temperance, but he knew a man who could draw a beer.

---

[30]Holden, "Frontier Journalism"; *Frontier Echo*, various issues.
[31]Fort Griffin *Echo*, Jan. 4, 1879.   [32]Ibid., June 14, 1879.

In general, his attitude was live-and-let-live. His advocacy of law and order applied to major crimes which affronted or threatened the community as a whole. It did not necessarily extend to illegal activities in which everyone engaged, or which didn't seem to bother anyone. For example:

> Jim Draper, Paul Hoffle and Si Able were each fined ten dollars for gaming. Can it be these gentlemen were selected for the purpose of "making an example" of? It is well known that gaming has been going on in this place ever since the first house was built and no one "kicked." It may be all right but it looks bad to "yank" the boys without giving them notice that the law would be enforced.[33]

Robson was known to turn a card or two himself. And while local enforcement of the gambling laws roused his ire, the antics down in Austin caused him to rear up in righteous indignation.

> The legislature is considering a bill to prevent playing poker-dice. Let it enact a law to prevent anyone from being out without their mother's knowledge, and then it would be in order to pass a joint resolution asking Providence to grant the law-makers sense enough to get home.[34]

The language of a modern newspaper may have changed, but the message has remained the same over the last hundred years.

Robson's patience with citizens could wear thin as well. When a person or family incurred his wrath, he let them know about it. Quoting from the Dodge City *Times*, he vented his anger on a local family, with which he had some sort of dispute.

> A young fellow by name of Amos Quitter was drowned at the bridge yesterday morning. He came up from Texas

[33]Ibid.
[34]Ibid., Feb. 12, 1881.

with the cowboys and while attempting to cross the rising Arkansas he went whizzing into eternity. He has a large number of relatives to mourn his fate. His body was not recovered being carried away by the raging stream. A large number of his relatives reside in Fort Griffin and vicinity and we can only wish that the whole family had gone to Kansas with the cowboys and been "whizzed into eternity by the raging waters of the Arkansas."[35]

Robson also had a running feud with Edgar Rye, who among his many other activities, published the Albany *Sun*. The quarrel reached the pages of both papers, and sometimes degenerated into pettiness.[36]

Still, G.W. Robson was the voice of the Flat. Through him, the long dead names appearing on court records, ledger sheets and Masonic rolls take on flesh and blood and become human beings. In the pages of the two *Echos*, we learn of their hopes, fears and aspirations, and find they were no different from us, a century later.

---

[35]Ibid., Aug. 20, 1880.
[36]Holden, *Frontier Journalism*, p. 216.

11

Life Among the
Law Abiding

In its early days, Albany was a bedroom town for
Fort Griffin. The Flat was a little too rough a place for
decent people to settle and raise a family. Young Henry
Herron's first impression of Fort Griffin was of "the
toughest place I had ever seen," when his father took
the family there in the fall of 1875. They camped at
Griffin only a week before John Herron heard of the
new town going up at Albany and moved them there.[1]

Mrs. H.C. Smith's experiences at the Occidental
Hotel were typical of those encountered by respectable
people in the Flat. "My Boarders," she wrote, "would
be (the) kind that was (in) a frontier town...Men
would get drunk when my husband would be gone
after supplies to Fort Worth(.) they would not alow a
drunken man to come in the Dining Room. I would not
go in town after Dark."[2] Considering that a round trip
to Fort Worth or Dallas might take from three weeks
to a month, depending on the weather, the experience
could be harrowing to a frontier wife left alone.

Still, Fort Griffin had law abiding citizens. In fact, it

---

[1]J.R. Webb, "Henry Herron."
[2]Mrs. H.C. Smith to Miss Mattie Anderson

is ironic that a town most noted for its saloons and drunken brawls would organize a branch of the Royal Templars of Temperance not long after its founding in Buffalo, New York, in 1870.[3] Like any organization, the temperance movement had its ups and downs. There were times when membership was enthusiastic, and there were times it lay dormant. But as long as it lasted, which was most of the life of the Flat, the movement was tolerated. G.W. Robson, himself no friend of the teetotalling crowd, reported on one such meeting, when enthusiasm was low:

> Rev. Dr. Young, chief of the temperence movement in Texas, lectured on his favorite subject Monday night in the school house, but failed to create sufficient interest among his hearers to induce them to organize a temperence council, however, the audience showed its liberality by contributing handsomely to defray the doctor's expenses.[4]

The "school house" in question was the Masonic Hall of Fort Griffin Lodge No. 489 AF & AM, a substantial stone building which has the only set of walls still standing from the glory days of the Flat. The Masonic fraternity was much stronger in the 19th Century than it is now, and most community leaders in Texas were members of the local lodge. It was particularly popular in military towns such as Fort Griffin, since the lodge was a place where officers and enlisted men met as equals in fraternal affiliation.

Until it was modified in the 1920s, the lodge hall was a two-story building ideal for community gatherings. It was used as a school with such regularity that it was generally called the "stone school house." Religious groups also borrowed it for their meetings.

There were several active religious organizations in

---

[3]Grant, p. 95.
[4]Fort Griffin *Echo*, May 31, 1879.

Fort Griffin. By mid-1879, the Methodists were already well-established, and the Rev. A.A. Hilliard, a Baptist missionary, was holding services in the lodge-school.[5] That same year, a Christmas party was held there, with a tree, Santa Claus, and presents for the children. A benefit supper raised funds for seats for the communal church, and a dance was held. Christmas was always a major event for families of the Flat. By early December, Frank Conrad, and Dr. Lignoski, the whiskey-vending druggist, would announce a line of Christmas toys.[6]

Another big day was the Fourth of July. Fort Griffin existed during the years of the American Centennial, and was caught up in the patriotic fervor of the period. Grudges from the War Between the States were forgotten. Citizens who had fought in butternut-grey celebrated with blue-coated soldiers from Government Hill, while small boys popped "that invention of the devil and a Chinaman, known s fire-crackers. A representative of the ECHO spent the day looking for men who were taking in the good old 4th but succeeded in finding but two, and judging from their queer actions and incoherent speech, they did not stop at the fourth but had certainly arrived at the twentieth drink."[7]

The 1879 celebration was so cordial that the *Echo* itself was slightly amazed.

> It is believed by many good people living in older states, that a gathering of the people on a public day is a failure in Texas unless a number of men are killed but it is a fact, not one
> ### PISTOL SHOT WAS FIRED
> in Fort Griffin or Albany yesterday.

---

[5]Ibid., July 17, 1879.
[6]Ibid., Dec. 13, 1879.
[7]Ibid., July 5, 1879.

> This country was at one time the home of thieves and
> desperados, but happily that day has passed. A more orderly,
> law abiding, intelligent, hard-working people than the in-
> habitants of Shackelford county, would be hard to find.[8]

Fort Griffin was reforming. In fact, only a few days
after this particular celebration, a mass meeting was
set to declare that Shackelford was no longer a frontier
county, and to urge a ban on the carrying of handguns.
However, the *Echo* countered that it was "improper and
impulsive" to pass such a law for the county.[9] It hadn't
reformed that much.

Politics always found enthusiasts among the men of
the Flat. Like virtually every other county in Texas at
the time (and many of them now), Shackelford was
solidly Democratic. In the 1876 presidential election,
Fort Griffin posted a "handsome majority" for Democrat Samuel Tilden in his race against Rutherford
Hayes.[10] On August 9 of that year, "qualified Democratic voters" from Shackelford and the surrounding
counties gathered in the Flat to name delegates to the
Democratic Congressional Convention set for August
30 in Dallas. The list of officers and delegates reads like
a *Who's Who* of the area. Hank Smith was named chairman, and J.W. Myers, secretary. Henry Jacobs was delegate for Precinct 1; W.H. Ledbetter, Precinct 2, and
George Mathews, J.N. Masterton and C.K. Stribling
for Precinct 4. Even John Larn was included, having
been named delegate for Precinct 3, which also covered
Throckmorton County.

The main item of business was the congressional
nomination. "A motion was unanimously adopted in-
structing the delegation to support Hon. J.W. Throck-

---

[8]Ibid.   [9]Ibid., July 15, July 26, 1879.
[10]Fort Worth *Democrat*, Nov. 8, 1876.

morton in the nominating convention *first, last and all the time* [*Frontier Echo's* emphasis]."[11]

Then, as now, there was nothing like a disaster to pull people together. And saints and sinners alike stood shoulder to shoulder in the Flat's worst disaster, the flood of 1879. Located as it was, on a river bottom, the Flat had seen floods before. In July 1870, when the town had barely gotten started, Collins Creek had overflowed. Again in June 1876, the Clear Fork filled up, water backed up in the creek and flooded the town. But no lives were lost and property damage was negligible. The flood of 1879 was different.[12]

The Clear Fork Valley is subject to alternating periods of extreme drought and torrential rains.[13] The late 1870s had been the dry spell which had caused John Irwin so much worry until John Larn gave him money for cattle feed. Now, as the summer of 1879 rolled around, the drought finally broke. Heavy rains had fallen intermittently throughout the day on June 20, but none had lasted more than an hour. However, at 8 p.m. a downpour began and the Signal Service officer stationed in the Flat recorded four inches of water within the next 90 minutes. The Clear Fork was reaching the top of its banks when a water-laden cloud burst at the head of Collins Creek, sending a wall of water down toward the river. Unable to flow into the Clear Fork, the creek overflowed at its weakest bank, behind Conrad and Rath's. A few minutes before ten, Caleb Cupp and a man identified as "Mr. Brown" ran through town firing their pistols to sound the alarm. Behind

[11]Jacksboro *Frontier Echo*, Aug. 18, 1876.

[12]Fort Griffin *Echo*, June 28, 1879.

[13]Gus L. Evans, "Geology of Lambshead Ranch," addendum to Frances Mayhugh Holden, *Lambshead Before Interwoven*, p. 171.

them came the water, carrying everything movable in its path.

Up on Government Hill, Captain Irvine, commander of the garrison, sent a squad with a wagon and six mules to help move families who were flooded out. Buildings at the post were converted into temporary shelters.

John William Poe and a man named Trask carried a rope across the intersection of Griffin Avenue and Fourth Street to serve as a lifeline for women and children trying to escape to high ground. By now the water was three feet deep and rushing down the street with such force that it knocked them off their feet several times. They finally reached Gus Huber's saloon on the opposite corner, but the slack of the rope was caught up in the current. Four strong men hauled it out. "By the aid of this rope," the *Echo* reported, "a number of women and children...were assisted to places of safety."[14]

J.W. Wray, the attorney who had tried to get John Larn out on bail a year before, was awakened to find the water waist deep inside his house. He made his way to the well outside, where he cut the bucket rope and threw one end of it to his wife. Then he got to a pecan tree, climbed it and hauled her to safety. The Wrays stayed in the tree until daylight, when a table and a bathtub drifted past. Poe was nearby, and together he and Wray placed the bathtub in the upended table, and the Wrays climbed in. Poe remained in the water, steering the makeshift boat to safety.

Poe almost drowned trying to help Miss Willie Reed across a low spot between Cupp's hardware store and the bakery. The current caught them and swept them

---

[14]Fort Griffin *Echo*, June 28, 1879.

down the street, carrying them through town and banging them against buildings and debris. Cut and bruised, they finally came up against a telegraph pole by the hill, where Poe grabbed hold and managed to pull them out.

The rushing water knocked out the north wall of the telegraph office, and flooded Conrad and Rath's, Mrs. Northwood's boarding house, Charley Meyers' general store, and farther down the street, his saloon. It ran through Cupp's "like a millrace," scoured out Louis Wolfrom's bakery, and undermined the foundations of the old tannery building. Most of the downtown business district was flooded out, although York's and Frankel's were on high ground and came through with relatively minor damage.

Hardest hit was the low ground by the Clear Fork, where the prostitutes lived in their shanties. Indian Kate Gambel lived on a fill in a ravine, directly in the path of the water. The flood cut all around her, leaving the house intact, but perched on an island. Louis Villipigne had gone down to lead the girls to safety. He was carrying Lizzie Hardin's six-year-old son and towing her by the arm when the water hit. Lizzie managed to catch hold of a tree limb behind Indian Kate's and hung on until Kate could climb out the back window and reach for her with a broom handle, hauling Lizzie to safety. Villipigne and the little boy were not so lucky. The current swept Villipigne down the street until he finally tangled up in a mesquite tree and was rescued, more dead than alive. The body of Lizzie's son was found three-quarters of a mile beyond.

Eventually, the floodwaters receded and the Flat set about cleaning up and burying its dead. Lizzie's occupation was temporarily forgotten as Griffinites joined in mourning her son. Five days later, the body of a man about 20 years old was found floating in the creek behind the *Echo* office.[15] He was identified as the son of General J.J. Byrne, war hero and former U.S. marshal, who himself was to die a year later in the Victorio War in West Texas.[16] Young Byrne had been camped on the creek about half a mile above town, with two ox wagons belonging to Henry Jacobs. "Man, wagons, oxen and a horse were swept away and drowned," the *Echo* reported. The body was claimed by Frank Conrad, who provided for a funeral at his own expense.

Looking back on it a week later, the *Echo* reported:

As evidence of the great
VOLUME AND FORCE OF THE WATER
which swept over the town, one only had to look at the wagons carried hundreds of feet, coils of fence wire and boxes of farm machinery carried across the street, rock fences torn to pieces and some of the stone found hundreds of yards away, huge piles of lumber floated off and when found, still nicely stacked...
Four thousand dollars would not be an over estimate of the loss sustained.[17]

That was a princely sum in a time when Lyman Bridges of Chicago offered a pre-fab, seven-room frame home for $1,850, and a frame store building from the same firm was $800.[18]

As with other crises, the Flat bounded back, and viewed the world with unabashed optimism. Already, G.W. Robson was editorializing for a high school in Fort Griffin, saying,

---

[15]Ibid.

[16]Charles M. Robinson III, *Frontier Forts of Texas*, p. 57.

[17]Fort Griffin *Echo*, June 28, 1879.

[18]Editors of Time-Life Books with Keith Wheeler, *The Old West—The Townsmen*, pp. 28-29.

It is a matter of vital importance to many of our most respected citizens who have children to educate. The prosperity and business importance of the town would be aided more by starting a first class school than any other enterprise. It would draw a better class of immigrants to settle with us. We have a central location; the boarding facilities, a commodius building, an abundance of good water as well as all the necessary natural advantages. Who will be the first to make the start in this laudable undertaking?[19]

It would have seemed easy enough. There were already a literary society and a reading club, and the former sponsored regular debates. But the debates often degenerated into quarrels, which may in the long run have hindered the community.[20] After all, Texans have long memories. Still, the Flat had a literate population, which was profoundly interested in the world around it. Citizens subscribed to newspapers and magazines from New York and London. In both Jacksboro and Fort Griffin, Robson got much of his national and international news this way. Considering the time and place, Griffinites were very urbane.[21]

And so life went on. The Rev. Ezell, a Presbyterian minister from Weatherford, held meetings in Albany, Fort Griffin, Camp Cooper and Buffalo Gap. The circuit-riding schedule could pretty well be determined by the fact that Baptists met the fourth Sunday of the month; Methodist-Episcopalians (South), the first Sunday; and Presbyterians, the second Sunday.[22]

But there were signs of decline. On February 12, 1881, the *Echo* announced the Free White School would close in six days. However, the teacher, J.R. Lewis,

---

[19]Fort Griffin *Echo*, March 1, 1879.
[20]Grant, p. 103.
[21]Jacksboro *Frontier Echo*, Fort Griffin *Echo*, various issues, 1875-1881.
[22]Fort Griffin *Echo*, Dec. 6, 1879, Jan. 29, 1881.

would offer private school through summer. Lewis's "Fort Griffin Academy" announced its first honor roll on April 16. Tuition was $2 a month for primary classes, $2.50 for intermediate, and $3 for academic.[23]

In fact, the Flat was dying, and it had been dying for a long time. But before it passed from history into legend, it had one final fling, a boom which threatened even the mighty Fort Worth.

---

[23]Ibid., Feb. 12, 1881, Apr. 16, June 11, 1881.

12

The Cowboys
Come to Town

The Great Western Cattle Trail ran in some form or other from Brownsville, north across Texas and the Indian Territory to Dodge City, Kansas. Along the whole route Texas cattle poured in from feeder trails, especially along the "trunk" or main trail which started about Bandera. This trail ran in an imprecise line along a general route, varying a few miles east or west as the cattle followed the best forage. But regardless of variances, it always put the cowboys within easy riding distance of Fort Griffin.[1]

This could not have been more convenient for the businessmen of the Flat. Even as the buffalo hide industry was at its height, they knew they were dealing with a limited resource, whose days were numbered. As early as 1876, Jacksboro's *Frontier Echo* reported that 50,000 head of cattle had come through the Flat in one four-week period near the opening of the season.[2] Accordingly, the businessmen began shifting to a new

[1]Jimmy M. Skaggs, "The Great Western Cattle Trail to Dodge City, Kansas," M.A. thesis, Texas Technological College, pp. 24-25, hereinafter referred to as "The Great Western."

[2]*Frontier Echo*, May 12, 1876.

clientele. Whereas, Frank Conrad and Charley Rath had previously prided themselves in supplying hunters, their advertising would ultimately proclaim, "Drovers Outfitting Goods A Specialty."[3]

In the first years of the trailing industry, drovers followed the older, more proven Chisholm Trail. It also had its roots near Brownsville, then went up through Belton and Fort Worth to Kansas markets such as Abilene, Wichita and Ellsworth. But as Central Texas was given more to farming, with the accompanying fences and boundary markers, and as the Kansas legislature extended its quarantine westward, more and more cattlemen looked for a trail farther west.

Since the quarantine had such an impact on the trailing industry, a word of explanation is in order. Texas cattle had long been suspected of carrying some sort of plague, and in 1858, the Kansas legislature took action to control it. But the real impact was not felt until after the War Between the States, when the great drives began. The tough Texas longhorns grew and prospered, but everywhere they passed, shorthorn cattle sickened and died. Few people at that time suspected the fever was carried by a specific type of tick (boophilus bovis), but everyone realized something was wrong. And whatever the reason, the evidence pointed back to cattle from Texas. Over the centuries, they had become immune to the fever, and could carry the ticks northward with no ill effects to themselves. Wherever the ticks dropped and reattached themselves to shorthorns, the latter animals almost invariably died. Regardless of cause, Kansas tightened up its regulations and began quarantining whole portions of the state. In 1876, the entire area east of Ford County was closed to

---

[3]Fort Griffin *Echo*, Jan 4, 1879.

Texas cattle. Since Dodge City was in Ford County, it became the only legal railhead available for the southern herds.[4] And Dodge City was due north of Fort Griffin. Thus the Flat became the intermediate supply point. Each outfit camped a day and a night nearby, to stock up with enough provisions to get them to the next depot, which was Doane's Store on the Red River.

Eighteen-seventy-six was the first big year for the Great Western and for Fort Griffin as far as cattle were concerned. From then on, the town enjoyed a new boom that picked up the slack as the hide industry began to taper off. The cowboys came to town and the Flat welcomed them with qualified tolerance.

Typical was this report:

> It was rather amusing to see that cow boy sitting on his horse in the middle of the street in front of York's Store Monday. A colored man held the horse by the bit while the rider played the "Arkansas Traveler" on a fiddle. The horse did not seem to appreciate the music but the crowd did.[5]

Hidden under the amusement and avarice was genuine concern about the way cowboys handled themselves in town. It might seem odd that a place like Fort Griffin would worry about proprieties. But the Flat had enough problems with its own random brawls and killings, and didn't need any extra worries riding in from South Texas. If, from time to time, a man was murdered over a soiled dove, or if a buffalo hunter or a couple of soldiers occasionally blazed away with their weapons, that was one thing. A band of cowboys out to tree a town was quite another. Besides, as the decade drew to a close, Griffinites were becoming concerned about

---

[4]Jimmy M. Skaggs, *The Cattle Trailing Industry, Between Supply and Demand, 1866-1890,* pp. 103-109.

[5]Fort Griffin *Echo,* June 7, 1879.

their reputation in the outside world. Thus, notices such as this one began appearing with increasing frequency:

TO THE COWBOYS

After spending weeks and often months on the range, a natural desire takes possession of many of you, to visit town, shave, clean up, put on new clothes, get "biling drunk," fire your six-shooter and raise the devil generally. You think this is fun, but you violate the laws of the State when you get drunk, yell like a Comanche, fire your pistol or in any manner make loud or boisterous noises, calculated to disturb the peace of quiet citizens.

Our citizens are always glad to see you come to town but they do not like to see you get into rows or disturb the peace.

Several of you have been punished this week for violating the laws, although most of you injured no one and had no thoughts of harm when you violated the laws; you damn the Mexican and ape him by running your horses and firing your guns and pistols, just to hear them roar; you despise the half-naked, lousy Indian and then try to mimic his unearthly yell; your conduct is often anything but gentlemanly still you want to and intend to conduct yourselves as such and are quick to resent a doubt even, that you are not.

Many of the stock raisers come to town, get tight and have what they think is fun and lots of it, too, but seldom do you see one of them down, or hear him yell or fire his pistol. Why cannot you do the same?

...We always like to see you and are sorry for you when you get into trouble, but you know that nine times out of ten, you bring on the trouble...

Come to town as often as you want to boys, stay as long and drink as much mean whisky as you can and enjoy yourselves in any way you please, but do not do those things which you know are likely to make trouble for yourselves.[6]

Things could be rough. G.O. Burrow, who worked for Jim Browning (later lieutenant governor) near Fort

---

[6]Ibid., July 19, 1879.

Griffin, said, "I had my times running out of saloons and gambling houses when some fool would start to shooting."[7]

According to Edgar Rye, the morning after a drunk "was the critical time, when there was almost sure to be a clash between the scape graces and the officers."[8] One such fight developed after the Gamble outfit had spent the night whooping it up in the saloons and dance halls of the Flat. About 8 a.m., the drovers stumbled back to retrieve their horses at Hank Smith's wagon yard, then headed to the Beehive for a farewell drink. While they were at it, Dick Bell, the black cook, himself two hundred pounds and tough, rode in to tell them the herd was ready to move.

The Gamble outfit had a reputation from the previous year. Deputy Dave Barker suspected they might exit by riding through the town at a gallop, firing their pistols at anything that moved. He took three heavily armed citizens and hid in a mesquite thicket down by the river at the foot of Griffin Avenue. Just as he suspected, the cowboys charged through town, the cook among them. But as they neared the thicket, they caught on and veered off to another trail. Bell, on a slower mount, had lost sight of them and stayed on the main trail. When he reached the thicket, Barker ordered him to surrender. Bell answered with a gunshot, then wheeled around and headed back up the avenue with the posse in hot pursuit. Shots flew back and forth, until Bell's horse was killed. He crawled behind it and used it as a breastwork until Ed Forrest emptied a load of buckshot into him.

Despite all the gunplay, only one member of the

[7]J. Marvin Hunter, *The Trail Drivers of Texas*, p. 674.
[8]Rye, p. 284.

posse was hurt, and that was a flesh wound. Bell wasn't as lucky. He had been wounded eleven times, including the blast of buckshot, and was not expected to live. A black family took him in and nursed him, and within two weeks, he was back on the trail again.[9]

But Griffinites were not total innocents. Shackelford County was the last organized county on the trail, and herds had to be inspected at the crossing of the Clear Fork. As we saw with John Larn and John Selman, fraudulent inspectors made a racket of charging permit fees from drovers who were in a hurry. Drover John Young recalled one such incident when three purported "cattle inspectors" demanded $325 for a health certificate to let his herd pass. When Young wanted to see their authorization, they threatened to have the army impound the herd. Young challenged them to call the troops. This apparently took them by surprise, and after consulting among themselves, the "inspectors" offered to pass the herd for only $100. "I knew that they were dead beats," Young said. "I did not pay a cent and had no trouble getting the herd away."[10]

In addition to the cattle coming up the trail, Shackelford County itself was becoming a center for livestock raising. G.W. Robson, editor of the *Echo*, wrote of some of the area's stockraisers during his account of a hunting trip with Frank Conrad. They spent the first night with Budd and Sallie Mathews, whose family partnership controlled about 15,000 head. The next day, they stopped off in Throckmorton County, where the Millett Brothers and Irwin partnership had "not far from 40,000 head," and employed some forty men to work them. They had just sent 3,200 head to New Mexico

---

[9]Ibid., pp. 285-288.
[10]Hunter, p. 665; J. Frank Dobie, *A Vaquero of the Brush Country*, pp. 136-137.

under contract, and had just bought 2,500 cattle from South Texas.

"They are constantly driving off on contract and buying more," Robson said. "They never drive on the open market."[11]

Oddly enough, sheep were catching hold in Shackelford County as well, and seemed to be accepted without the resistance found elsewhere. The ever adaptable Fort Griffin business and ranching community had recognized wool as a new way to make money. In fact, a large portion of the $39,815 paid for wool in Fort Worth in June 1879 went to shippers in the Flat.[12]

Always one to boost the Flat and the livestock industry, Robson ran the following house ad in his *Echo*:

> We pride ourselves on being the only publisher who has been represented at *every meeting* [*Echo*'s emphasis] of the North-west Texas Stock Raisers Association, and believe we know more about stock and stock marks and brands than any publisher in North-west Texas.
>
> Believing that the Live Stock interest (and by this we mean *all* [*Echo*'s emphasis] kinds of stock raised for profit from the cow brute down to chickens,) of this portion of Texas is sufficient to warrant the publication of a paper in the Stock Interest, and believing the Range the proper location, THE ECHO has been moved to this point. It proposes to make the
>
> Live Stock Business
>
> a leading feature, but not to the exclusion of local and general news.[13]

Fort Griffin's enthusiasm was rewarded. In 1878, the North West Cattle Raiser's Association had its convention there. It was perhaps the Flat's greatest

---

[11]Fort Griffin *Echo*, June 21, 1879.

[12]Ibid., June 24, 1879.

[13]Ibid., June 14, 1879.

moment. The town was flooded with members. It was important enough to bring a reporter from the venerable *Galveston News*. As Rye later wrote:

> The word cosmopolitan but poorly expresses the nature of the conglomerate mixture of nationality and kindred tongues, of that great throng as it moved up and down the rows of saloons and restaurants like a herd of wild steers in a small corral.
>
> Hotels, restaurants, saloons, stores and wagon-yards did a thriving business and were crowded beyond their capacity, and any old place was good enough if it afforded room to spread a pair of blankets.
>
> Nothing like this convention had ever been conceived, much less actually announced to take place on the frontier. And it had been looked forward to somewhat in the spirit that takes possession of children as they anticipate the coming of Christmas. Hundreds of miles had been traveled and hundreds of dollars saved up for the occasion. And now there was to be a glorious realization of their fondest anticipations, and an event to look back to for many years to come.[14]

"There was a big crowd in town and of course the two hotels run by Jack Swartz [sic] and Jule Hervey were full as also were the two wagon yards," Phin Reynolds added. "The four big mercantile stores run by Frank Conrad, F.P. York, Charley Meyers, and E.E. Frankel were turned into sleeping quarters. These merchants took blankets out of their stock of merchandise which were furnished the visitors without charge and they slept on the counters and on the floors of the stores."[15]

The convention itself was held August 20 and 21. The new Masonic Lodge was furnished with seating for the members of the association, and tables, chairs and stationery for the officers. C.L. (Kit) Carter of

[14]Rye, pp. 288-289.
[15]P.W. Reynolds to J.R. Webb.

Cedar Creek in Palo Pinto County was nominated as president. He asked that his name be withdrawn, since he said he did not have time to serve. The man who nominated him replied "Well, I don't think, you will be elected anyway." The crowd had a good laugh and elected Carter.[16]

Like any convention, this one drew a rough element. "These boys were there to have the time of their lives, while the bosses attended to business, and a rip-rousing old time they had, too," Rye wrote.[17] Deputies Henry Herron and Dave Barker had been told to stay in the Flat and keep order. This made them targets for Zeno Hemphill, a gunslinger from the Double Mountain Fork of the Brazos, up near Aspermont. Phin Reynolds called Hemphill the type who "seemed to glory in a saloon fight." He appeared to have one great ambition in life, and that was to kill a lawman. Accordingly, he conspired with some South Texas cowboys to create an incident which would bring the deputies running.[18]

Someone tipped off the lawmen. According to Herron, Barker "proposed that we should be on the alert for their first move or until they made a break and then let them have it . . . I said, 'Maybe we can arrest them without any shooting and that if we could, that was the way to do it, to take them alive if we could.'"

That night, Hemphill's gang was in Jones and Rush's saloon. The big barroom was packed with people, so that the two deputies were able to slip in unnoticed. Barker pointed out the cowboys, and Herron took advantage of the crowd to ease over next to Hemphill.

---

[16]Ibid.,

[17]Rye, p. 289.

[18]The incident with Zeno Hemphill was related to J.R. Webb by P.W. Reynolds and Henry Herron, in the J.R. Webb Papers. Quotes of actual conversation are from Henry Herron, who was there.

Meanwhile, Barker stood by, keeping an eye on the others. Suddenly, Hemphill made his move. He hit one of the saloon girls in the face, knocking her back into the crowd. As he did, Herron drew his gun, grabbed Hemphill's from his holster, knocked him in the head with a pistol "and collared him." At the same time, Barker pulled his gun on the others and said, "I will kill the first man that makes a move." The South Texas cowboys had no intention of moving. This was Hemphill's fight, not theirs, and they watched quietly as Herron and Barker marched him to jail.

Hemphill had a nasty cut and was bleeding badly, but otherwise he was unhurt. Herron jailed him and sent for a doctor. The next day, he paid his fine and was turned loose. A short time later, Phin Reynolds saw him "sitting off to himself near the Clear Fork with a badly swollen head and face and the blood unwashed dried over him. He looked kind of pitiful."

He didn't spend much time feeling sorry for himself. Soon he rode up to a saloon, tied his horse out front and gave notice he intended to kill Dave Barker, then ride out of town. Barker had enough. He and Herron went over to the saloon, where he walked up to Hemphill and said, "I hear you are going to kill me and ride out of town."

"Well, I was going to do that, but I changed my mind," Hemphill replied.

"Now, Zeno, you get on your horse and you ride out of town and don't you ever come back," Barker ordered.

Hemphill complied and that was the last the Flat ever saw of him. Two or three years later, he was killed in a gunfight on saloon row in Abilene, Texas. He took a lawman and a saloon keeper with him into eternity.

13

Fort Worth
Strikes Back

Today, a couple of truck stops along a busy interstate
highway can turn a desert crossroads into a thriving
community. In the 19th Century, a cattle trail had the
same impact. Towns rose and fell according to the
strength and route of the drives. As long as cattle came
up the Chisholm, the prosperity of places like Fort
Worth and Belton was assured. Ranchers estimated it
cost about 60 cents a head to drive a marketable animal
every 1,500 miles. Thus a 2,500-head herd would cost
$1,500 or a dollar a mile. Almost 80 percent of this
total was disbursed in localities north of the point of
origin.[1] In a drive that could reach a quarter million
head or better in a season, the economic benefits to
trail towns were enormous. If anything were ever to
interfere, these towns could face disaster. And by 1875,
it was beginning to look like there might be problems
on the Chisholm.

Where the ranchers went, the farmers followed.
And with farmers came fences. Barbed wire was introduced into Texas in 1875, making it practical to fence
large areas for fields and pastures. Still the herds

---

[1]Skaggs, "The Great Western," pp. 86-87.

poured into Fort Worth. Then came the rails, and in 1877, Fort Worth shipped its first carload of refrigerated beef. It seemed like Kansas might not even be needed, and that the drives would terminate without leaving the state.[2]

By the Fort Worth *Democrat*'s estimate, seven-eighths of the entire 1877 drive passed through that city on the Chisholm.[3] There was no reason to feel the 1878 season would be any different. On April 9, 1878, the *Democrat* confidently announced that the season's first two herds, one with 2,700 head, and the other with 3,000, were headed toward Fort Worth.

> From information which the DEMOCRAT has been able to gather from various sources, the cattle drive for this year will be much larger than last season, and on account of the forward opening and early grass, the work will commence two or three weeks earlier. The good results derived from shipments during the past season, and the advantage which those enjoyed who shipped rather than drove their cattle to northern markets will have a tendency to increase shipments by rail. This will insure the advantage of this city which is now conceded to be the best shipping point in the State.[4]

This was premature. Rail transportation was more expensive than trailing and the cowboys still had to contend with the grangers who had set up their farms along the Chisholm. The Kansas quarantine clinched it. Faced with all these problems, the drovers took the simplest way out—the Great Western through Fort Griffin.

The first Chisholm Trail town to feel the pinch was Belton. During the 1877 season, Fort Griffin businessmen had "tapped the main trail to Belton, and by a good

[2]Wayne Gard, *The Chisholm Trail*, pp. 215-216, 234.
[3]Fort Worth *Democrat*, Apr. 18, 1878.
[4]Ibid., Apr. 9, 1878.

deal of hard labor, successed in diverting a good many thousand cattle from the Fort [Worth] to Fort Griffin," The *Democrat* reported:

> The success which attended their efforts the first season, spurred them on to greater achievements, and from the commencement of the present spring drive the merchants and business men have paid a man liberally to make his headquarters at Belton and induce the drivers to take the Griffin route. He sets forth the claim that the range is poor on the old drive, and that in not a few instances the trail is intercepted with fences and farms, the result of the progress and march of civilization. He claims more water, better grass, etc., and to many of those who do not know to the contrary, he easily induces them to follow his advice.
>
> This through drive is worth thousands of dollars to any city, and that our merchants should have lost sight of the importance of having a representative to offset the influence of Fort Griffin's enterprise at Belton is singular indeed.[5]

Belton saw the threat, and appealed to Fort Worth on the grounds that what hurt one would hurt the other. It was too late. By May 23, only 82,450 head had passed through Fort Worth, and the *Democrat* was estimating the season total at 102,450. On the other hand, Griffin had reported 150,000 head. The season was beyond salvage.

Looking back on the efforts of the Flat, the *Democrat* groused, "Had our businessmen been equally active in securing this immense drive, the season drive would not have fallen short of 200,000. Experience is a dear teacher. We hope that their eyes will be opened to their best interests next year."[6]

Fort Worth did learn. The next year, the local business community fielded trail agent Dave Blair to counter the Flat's representatives in Belton. Traveling

---

[5]Ibid., Apr. 18, 1878.
[6]Ibid., May 8, May 23, 1878.

throughout Southern Texas, he met the drovers on the trail or at their roundups, and urged them to come back. He sent his employers detailed letters, listing the cattlemen he had contacted, and the number and class of livestock in the herds.

"Have seen several of the drovers, and think I can safely promise your city near the entire drive this year," he reported.[7]

Inquiries started coming in. One man wrote, "As I will be one of the first to start from South Texas, I would be glad to have you write me more fully in regard to the Fort Worth trail. I will start about the 20th of March from Refugio county. I think all the cattle men aim to go on the old trail this year, if possible, as *no one* [*Democrat*'s emphasis] was pleased with the western trail that traveled it last year."

Another said, "We expect to arrive at the Fort on or about the 20th of April. I heard yesterday, that Dave Blair arrived in this part of the county."[8]

They came and Fort Worth breathed a sigh of relief. "The town is alive with the merry laugh and hilarious 'whoopla!' of the Texas cow-boy again. They all like to stop in the Fort," the *Democrat* reported.[9]

Blair might have been thorough, but not thorough enough. Grazing on the Great Western in fact was better, there was plenty of water and the range was still relatively free of fences. Fort Griffin's agents made sure everyone knew it. Now the cattle war began in earnest. G.W. Robson had been biding his time with the *Echo*, limiting his cattle reporting to statistical information. But when the *Democrat* said only three or

---

[7]Ibid., Feb. 26, 1879.
[8]Ibid., March 7, 1879.
[9]Ibid., Apr. 17, 1879.

four herds would pass through the Flat and the remainder would use Fort Worth, he rose to the challenge.

> Drovers will not take a route when they know they will be
> harrassed by small farmers claiming damages to fences and
> garden spots all along the trail; with lanes, on either side of
> which may be found a barbed wire fence; with innumerable
> things which tend to cause runs and stampedes, and loss of
> time and money, when there is open to them a route (via
> Fort Griffin,) free from all these vexations. Mr. Blair *may*
> [*Echo*'s emphasis] be correct in his opinion that more cattle
> from the South will be driven this year through Fort Worth
> than last, but that only three or four herds will travel the
> Fort Griffin route is "too thin."

The knife in, Robson gave it a twist.

> The ECHO is authorized to say that $500 or $1,000 will
> be put up and placed in a bank at Dallas or Fort Worth, to be
> covered by a like amount, that more cattle will be driven
> North from Southern Texas this year via Fort Griffin than
> via Fort Worth. The money is now on deposite [sic] with
> Conrad & Rath, merchants at this place. Talk is cheap and
> money scarce, so if the *Democrat*, Mr. Blair or any other man
> thinks he can make a winning on the cattle drive, just
> deposite [sic] your money and it will be promptly covered.[10]

Robson wasn't finished. In his next issue, he accused
Fort Worth's agents of completely misrepresenting
trail conditions on the Great Western. Brimming with
righteous indignation, he wrote, "It is right and proper
for the agents of Fort Worth to use all honorable
means to induce drovers to go that route, but it is not
right to misrepresent this or any other trail and if they
persist in circulating reports detrimental to any trail,
in the end they will be the loosers."

As if to emphasize the point, the same issue reported,

---

[10]Fort Griffin *Echo*, Apr. 19, 1879.

"This week two herds of cattle belonging to J.F. Ellison from Caldwell county, passed here, bound for Millett's range. The first contained 2,800 and the second 3,000 head, mostly young steers.

"Total drive to date: 8,050."[11]

This was a respectable number for so early in the season. But these were cattle bound for local ranges. The key to a successful season was through cattle, herds that were bound for Kansas or the Platte. The Flat's agents watched the herds along the trail and reported any positive activity. Transactions were carefully noted as to whether they involved through cattle.

Meanwhile, the two newspapers continued to feud. In an editorial entitled *Business vs. Bluff*, Robson wrote that the *Democrat* was trying to raise the ante on the number of cattle through Fort Worth. By setting the bet at $2,500, he said Fort Worth was trying to scare the Flat away from the deal. In response, Frank Conrad was ready to deposit $500 of his personal funds in a Dallas bank, on a bet against any man that Fort Worth would not get three-fourths of the drive.

"Give us the name of your man Mr. *Democrat* and the details will be reduced to writing. No bluff this," the *Echo* taunted.[12]

That was more than the *Democrat* could take.

PUT UP OR SHUT UP

snarled the headline in Fort Worth on May 10.

> ...we have been authorized to say by two prominent and responsible cattle men that they will only be too glad to accept the proposition of Mr. Conrad, in any sum from $500 up, that three-quarters of the Southern drive *will* [*Democrat*'s emphasis] cross the Trinity on the Fort Worth trail...

---

[11]Ibid., Apr. 26, 1879.
[12]Ibid., May 3, 1879.

Come now, pull down your vest, gentlemen, and "put up or shut up."[13]

PUT UP

was the Flat's response.

The Fort Worth *Democrat* has been authorized by two prominent and respectable cattlemen to accept Mr. Frank E. Conrad's proposition that three-fourths of the Southern cattle drive will not pass Fort Worth. Mr. Conrad was shown the acceptance yesterday at the county seat, where he is in attendance on district court, and he has requested THE ECHO to say, as soon as court is over he will return home and settle the controversy by depositing the money ($500) as per his proposition. The *Democrat* will please favor Mr. Conrad by sending him (by mail) as soon as possible the names of the two gentlemen.[14]

By late May, the herds were coming in at more than 20,000 head a week. On May 24, the total to date in Fort Griffin was 66,610. A week later it had reached 87,950. The drive through Fort Worth was 90,800 and 104,972, respectively, an increase of only 14,172 for the same period.

Commenting on this, the *Echo* said, "It is good for their pockets that those Fort Worth gentlemen did not come to time on that wager on the cattle drive. 'Fort Worth will have three to Fort Griffin one' was their proposition. Our reports to day show the total drive to be 192,922, three forths [sic] of which is 144,922. Griffin has 87,950 head, just double the number we are intitled to according to Fort Worth's estimate."[15]

The feud continued all summer. The two newspapers were in the thick of it. As it progressed, one almost

---

[13]Fort Worth *Democrat*, May 10, 1879.
[14]Fort Griffin *Echo*, May 17, 1879.
[15]Ibid., May 24, May 31, 1879.

suspects that Robson and the editor of the *Democrat* encouraged the rivalry and contrived incidents and insults, to keep interest up and thus sell more papers. Regardless of that, the cowboys kept coming and by early July, the Flat was "packed with cattlemen." A total of 120,275 head had come through by July 12.[16] When the season closed, more cattle had crossed the Trinity at Fort Worth than had crossed the Clear Fork of the Brazos at Fort Griffin. But not much more. And not enough to upstage the Flat. Fort Worth was struggling for its existence.

The year 1879 marked the last great drive on the Chisholm. From then on, until the end of the trailing industry in Texas, supremacy rested with the Great Western. The greatest year was 1884, after which it gradually declined until the last drive in 1894.[17] By then, it made no difference to either town. Fort Worth had become a major rail center, and for all practical purposes, the Flat no longer existed.

16Ibid., July 5, July 12, 1879.
17Skaggs, "The Great Western," p. 107.

14

The Fall of
Fort Griffin

Fort Griffin was doomed almost from the day it was founded. It was strictly a frontier town, and existed for frontier purposes. Its economy was based on the needs of a new, unsettled territory, and when the territory became settled, those needs no longer existed. The tripod which held it up consisted of the military, buffalo hunters and cattlemen. There were still some sporadic Indian raids, but by and large the plains tribes had been pacified. Thus the military became unnecessary. The destruction of the buffalo herds ended the hide trade. And finally, advances in the livestock and transportation industries combined with the expansion of farming to end the great cattle drives.

The buffalo hunters were the first to go. Their end came in the 1878-1879 season. Whereas three years earlier, a hunter could take as many as two thousand hides in the space of three or four months, now he was lucky to get a few hundred in half a year. The Mooars returned from the range in July 1879, with "nine wagons loaded with 1,400 buffalo hides and nearly 300 deer, antelope, wolf and other small skins."[1] But they

---

[1]Fort Griffin *Echo*, July 12, 1879.

were the exceptions. And even for them, this was the last great hunt. Almost all the others were small scale hunters, and they might as well have stayed home. Uncle Joe McCombs, who had started it all with that first hunt on Christmas Day 1874, went out for the last time in September 1878. Although he stayed on the range until March, he only took eight hundred hides. Looking back on it, he said:

> Buffalo were scarce and wild and started north on their very last migration before their usual time. But they never got back to their summer range. Hunters finished their existance as herds on the great ranges this spring of 1878, and all that remained of the vast herds of a few years back were a few straggling bunches, mostly calves. I do not recollect having seen a buffalo on the range after the return from my last hunt...There was no hunting after that.[2]

The collapse of the hide industry left a large segment of the population unemployed. To what extent this caused hardship seemed to depend on the individual. For those willing to endure the loneliness and privation, the hunt had been a way to make a lot of money in a relatively short period of time. Many Griffinites had tried their hands at it at one point or another. Some, like Henry Herron, Joe McCombs, John William Poe and Pat Garrett either settled down locally or moved away and went into other professions. The buffalo ranges seemed to be a training ground for law enforcement, since some of the more famous hunters later earned reputations as lawmen. Other hunters drifted off into the Indian Territory or to the Black Hills and were forgotten.

But there was a thug element among the hunters as

---

[2]"The Frontier Life of Uncle Joe S. McCombs," MS, Earl Vandale Collection, Eugene S. Barker Texas History Center.

well. These men had often fled to the buffalo ranges from trouble elsewhere, and had generally been the ones who had given the Flat its bad reputation. Now there were no buffalo to keep them busy, and they began to look for other ways to make fast money. The easiest way was usually illegal. Ex-hunters went up to the Comanche Agency at Fort Sill, traded their rifles and ammunition for horses and returned to Texas as cattle thieves. In fact, for some years after the hunt ended, the vast majority of thieves who harrassed the plains ranches were former hunters and skinners.[3]

But the Flat had already adjusted to the end of the hunt. Cattle were pouring in, and there was still the Army payroll. Then, on May 14, 1881, the *Echo* announced the end of the second leg of the economic tripod:

> Lieut. Getty, A.A.Q.M., at this post, has orders to sell a large quantity of government property, a considerable portion of it being valuable, and all the buildings of the garrison. Sale by auction, May 25th. This is a good opportunity for our sheep raiser to buy lumber for sheds & and we expect to see a number of them avail themselves of it."[4]

Six days after the sale, the soldiers were gone, and an era had come to a close.

> At sundown, May 31, 1881, the flag at the United States military post known as Fort Griffin, was taken down, never again to be unfurled over military forces at that place. The order had gone forth for the abandonment of the post, property had been removed to other storehouses, a large amount was condemned and sold, and the remainder was packed up and with the troops left on the above date for Fort Clark...The soldiers, taken as a body were a good set of

[3]Dobie, *A Vaquero of the Brush Country*, pp. 135-136.
[4]Fort Griffin *Echo*, May 14, 1881.

men, well behaved and well liked by our community, of course there were a few bad men, who made the officers, our county officers and citizens trouble.[5]

For fourteen years, the Army had been the mainstay of the community. It was not always a happy relationship, but it had been vital all the same. The town had sprung up to provide services to the soldiers, and the military was a steady source of income when times were lean. The Army sold some of the buildings for relocation or dismantling before the post was abandoned. The rest were allowed to stand as they were. Since the government had never actually owned the reservation, no one bothered to keep an eye on the remaining structures and most were soon dismantled. Edgar Rye, who witnessed the end of the Flat, recalled the mood when the fort was closed:

> All the business men, hotel men, saloon men and artisans in the Flat were hunting new locations, and an air of dejection pervaded the whole community.[6]

To Sallie Reynolds Mathews, the area seemed "rather deserted; we missed the life and stir of a military post..."[7]

With the Army gone, the Tonkawas presented an embarrassing situation. Quite simply, the government had no further use for them. But Griffinites were not willing to let them fade into oblivion. For all their rowdiness, drinking and tribal peculiarities, these tough little Indians had made themselves part of the community. During the height of the Comanche problems, some of them would camp out by the Mathews place whenever Joe B. was away from home, to make sure

---

[5]Ibid., June 4, 1881.
[6]Rye, p. 356.
[7]Sallie Reynolds Mathews, *Interwoven*, p 158.

the family would be protected.[8] The people of Shackleford County had grown fond of them and now rallied
to their defense.

Even before Fort Griffin was closed, a petition was
making its rounds, setting out "in strong language the
claims of recognition these Indians have upon the
people of Texas; of their many privations and sufferings
for and on account of their white bretheren; of shed-
ding their blood in war for the whites and how they
engendered the hatred of other tribes by so doing; how
they have been reduced by exposure and war . . ."

The petition asked the legislature to set aside funds
to purchase "not less than 3000 acres of land for them
and put them on it under an agent to be appointed by
the governor, from among the citizens of this county,
and the further sum of not less than $10,000 to fence in
their land (by wire); to build comforta[ble] quarters; for
buying farming implements; and to furnish them food
and raiment for the next two years, after which it is
thought they will be self-sustaining. This is a step that
should have been taken long ago. There is no tribe of
Indians that have as just claims upon the people as the
Tonks, and they have received less than all others. It is
hoped that the legislature will take hold of this matter
promptly and relieve these unfortunate creatures."[9]

If the people of Shackleford County saw the debt,
the legislature did not. No action was taken, and not
long after the post was closed, the Tonkawas were
removed to the Indian Territory.

Now, the Flat was truly dying. Cattle continued to
come in—175,229 head by June 18, 1881, with several
thousand more on the trail.[10] But more and more of

---

[8]Ibid., p. 112.
[9]Fort Griffin *Echo*, Feb. 5, 1881.   [10]Ibid., June 18, 1881.

the land was being given over to sheep, shorthorns and small farms. As Rye observed:

> A transformation was taking place on the range...and wire fencing was being used to fence in pastures and the homes of settlers were dotting the prairies, and there was little free grass left.
>
> Consequently, Albany began to take on new life and clamor for recognition among the towns of Northwest Texas.[11]

Even G.W. Robson was ready to throw in the towel. On Feb. 26, 1881, he put the *Echo* and its print shop up for sale, citing bad health and "business interests elsewhere which are of more importance to him than that in which he is engaged."[12] Later, he apparently changed his mind and decided to stay until the end. As usual, the *Echo* remained the best indicator of the goings-on in the Flat. And a newspaper's best economic barometer is its advertising. As 1881 turned into 1882, the big Conrad ads were gone. Frank Conrad himself moved his emporium into Albany. There were no more ads from Cupp's, and Frankel's were cut down. Whereas in years past, Robson almost invariably had something to say about Doc Lignoski, the whiskey-vending druggist, there was no more mention of him.

There was a glimmer of hope. A mineral well was discovered nearby, and the remaining citizens of the Flat made the most of it. Speculating on the possibilities of the mineral waters, Robson wrote, "It is expected that all the railroads now building in North Texas will center here, making this point a second Indianapolis and leave Kansas City in the shade." He urged his readers to subscribe to the *Echo* and "learn all about the

---

[11]Rye, p. 356.
[12]Fort Griffin *Echo*, Feb. 26, 1881.

big boom."[13] The boom never came, and by the end of the year, the *Echo* was gone too.

Now it was Albany's turn. Already holding the county seat, and having gone from bedroom city to commercial center, its citizens decided the time had come for a railroad. After an unsuccessful attempt to get the Texas and Pacific, they decided to go after Texas Central, which had extended its lines as far as Cisco. In a community-wide fund-raising, the people collected $50,000 to bring the rails into Albany, by-passing the Flat completely. The first train arrived on December 20, 1881, but went no farther for almost twenty years. Albany remained the western terminus until 1900, when Texas Central finally extended into Jones County.[14]

Albany never boomed, but it survived. Fort Griffin did not. The Flat dwindled away. In 1986, its population was listed as 96 persons in "scattered rural homes on Brazos River farmlands."[15] It would be hard to even find that. The only obvious remnant is the fort on Government Hill. The centerpiece of Fort Griffin State Historical Park, it consists of a few ruined buildings, foundations, a visitor center and some reconstructed barracks buildings. In the bottomland across the high-way, the old Ward Ranch house is now used by park rangers, and is the only building from the era which is intact. The ruins of York's store, erroneously identified for many years as Conrad's, stood in the Flat until well into the 1930s. Now, they are gone. The only walls remaining are those of the old Masonic Lodge which was the center of so many community activities. Aside

---

[13]Ibid., Jan. 14, 1882.
[14]Grant, pp. 145-147.
[15]*Texas Travel Handbook*, p. 58.

from that, one actually has to look for the Flat, and know what one is looking for, in order to see any trace of it. Here and there are foundation stones, which can be identified as this business or that. A long, narrow expanse of scrub grass, growing out of hard-packed soil devoid of the surrounding brush, marks the once-busy Griffin Avenue. and always there are the silent trees on the Clear Fork and Collins Creek, those same trees which held up many a body at the end of a rope.

The only visible legacies of Fort Griffin are the annual fandangle, held each June in Albany, and Fort Griffin Lodge No. 489, A.F.&A.M., which meets in Throckmorton. The cowboys, soldiers and buffalo hunters are gone. So is the quiet, respectable John Larn, who was perhaps one of the deadliest men ever to roam the West. Gone, too, are the gun-toting John Selman, the hard-drinking Doc Holliday and the mysterious Lottie Deno. They have passed out of history and into legend. And so has the tough frontier town which became such an important, and yet so little-known part of our Western heritage.

The last remaining building of the Flat, the ruins of Fort Griffin Lodge No. 489, A.F. & A.M., as it was in 1986. Courtesy author's collection.

Appendix

Dramatis Personae

The Army

BUELL, GEORGE B.: One of the commanding officers of Fort Griffin.

GRIFFIN, CHARLES: Military commandant of Texas under Reconstruction. Died of yellow fever on September 15, 1867. Fort Griffin was named for him.

LEE, ROBERT EDWARD: Commander of Camp Cooper in 1856-1857. Later became Confederate general.

MACKENZIE, RANALD SLIDELL: Commanding officer of the Fourth Cavalry, and later of the Military Department of Texas. Born, New York City, 1840. Died, Staten Island, 1889.

MARCY, RANDOLPH BARNES: Inspector general of the army.

MCCONNELL, H.H.: Sergeant of the Sixth Cavalry, stationed at Fort Richardson. Chronicled army life in the area.

SHERMAN, W.T.: General-in-chief of the army.

The Buffalo Hunters

MCCOMBS, JOE: Led the first hunt from Fort Griffin on Christmas Day, 1874.

MERRY, S.P.: Hunter operating out of Fort Griffin.

MOOAR, JOHN WESLEY: Headed one of the leading hunt operations in the west, with his brother, Wright.

MOOAR, JOSIAH WRIGHT: John Wesley Mooar's brother and partner. Born in Bennington County, Vermont, August 10, 1851. Organized the first large scale hunt out of Fort Griffin in 1875. Later settled in Snyder, Texas. Died, May 1, 1940.

WOODY, J.W.: Hunter operating out of Fort Griffin.

Leading Citizens

BROCK, JAMES A.: Cattleman and businessman. Spent years proving himself innocent of a murder.

CONRAD, FRANK EBEN: Fort Griffin merchant. Born in Rockford, Illinois, May 4, 1842. Came to Fort Griffin as post trader in 1870, and established leading mercantile emporium between Fort Worth and El Paso. Married Rose Ella Mathews, daughter of Joseph Beck Mathews and Caroline Spears. Died, Albany, May 4, 1892.

IRWIN, JOHN CHADBOURNE: Rancher and early settler in the Clear Fork Valley. Born at Fort Chadbourne, Texas, February 7, 1852. Moved with his family to Clear Fork area in 1859. Died February 17, 1938.

LARN, MARY JANE MATHEWS: Daughter of Joseph Beck Mathews and Caroline Spears. Married John M. Larn.

MATHEWS (MATTHEWS), JOHN ALEXANDER (BUDD): Son of Joseph Beck Mathews and Caroline Spears. Married Sallie Ann Reynolds.

MATHEWS, JOSEPH BECK: Leading rancher. Came to the Clear Fork in 1858. Married Caroline Spears.

MATHEWS, SALLIE ANN REYNOLDS: Daughter of Barber Watkins Reynolds and Anne Maria Campbell. Chronicled frontier life in book, *Interwoven*.

MEYERS, CHARLEY: Fort Griffin merchant and saloon keeper.

RATH, CHARLES: Hide shipper. One of Frank Conrad's partners.

REYNOLDS, BARBER WATKINS (WATT): Pioneer in the Clear Fork area. Married Anne Maria Campbell.

REYNOLDS, BENJAMIN FRANKLIN (BEN): Son of Barber Watkins Reynolds and Anne Maria Campbell. Married Florence Rebecca Mathews, niece of Joseph Beck Mathews.

REYNOLDS, GEORGE THOMAS: Son of Barber Watkins Reynolds and Anne Maria Campbell. Married Lucinda Elizabeth Mathews, daughter of Joseph Beck Mathews and Caroline Spears.

REYNOLDS, GLEN: Son of Barber Watkins Reynolds and Anne Maria Campbell. Probably involved in the killing of John Larn.

REYNOLDS, PHINEAS WATKINS (PHIN): Son of Barber Watkins Reynolds and Anne Maria Campbell. Married Roseannah Marion Mathews, niece of Joseph Beck Mathews.

ROBSON, G.W.: Editor of the Fort Griffin *Echo*. Originally established the *Frontier Echo* in Jacksboro in 1875. Moved the paper to Fort Griffin at the end of December, 1878.

RYE, EDGAR: Born in Kentucky, June 22, 1848. Newspaperman, poet and bon vivant. Came to Fort Griffin in 1875, and settled in Albany, where he ran the Albany *Sun*. Also served as justice of the peace. Died in Los Angeles, June 6, 1920.

SMITH, HENRY CLAY (HANK): Born in Germany as Heinz Schmidt. Orphaned at age 12, and immigrated to U.S. to live with sister. Came to Fort Griffin in 1871, and operated hay, wood and wagon yards, a hotel and other businesses. Moved to Crosby area, went into ranching in 1876.

SMITH, ELIZABETH BOYLE (AUNT HANK): Born in Ayrshire, Scotland, July 12, 1848. Went to Fort Griffin with her brothers in 1873. Married Hank Smith, May 19, 1874. Ran Smith businesses in Fort Griffin until 1878, when she followed her husband to Crosby.

YORK, F.B.: Fort Griffin merchant and outfitter.

The Law

ARRINGTON, G.W.: Commanded Company B, Frontier Battalion, Texas Rangers, in Larn Affair.

BARKER, DAVE: Deputy sheriff in Fort Griffin.

CAMPBELL, G.W.: Texas Ranger, succeeded Arrington as commander of the Company B in Larn Affair.

CRUGER, BILL: Chief deputy under John M. Larn, and succeeded him as sheriff in 1877. Probably involved in the killing of Larn. Resigned in 1880. Died in Albany, Georgia, December 29, 1882.

DRAPER, JIM: Deputy sheriff and vigilante. Killed Johnny Golden. Probably involved in the killing of John Larn.

GILSON, BILL: Fort Griffin town marshal. Involved in the killings of Johnny Golden and John Larn.

HERRON, HENRY: Buffalo hunter and lawman. Born, Wisconsin, December 16, 1855. Arrived in Albany with his family in 1875. Died, Albany, August 18, 1944.

JACOBS, HENRY: First sheriff of Shackelford County. Succeeded by John M. Larn in April 1876.

JACOBS, JOHN: Brother of Henry Jacobs. Succeeded Bill Cruger as sheriff in 1880.

JONES, JOHN B.: Commanding officer, Frontier Battalion, Texas Rangers. Did not personally participate in the Larn Affair but controlled movements of his Rangers at the time.

JONES, NEWTON JOSEPHUS (NEWT): Texas Ranger during the Larn Affair. Born in Elm Ridge, Kaufman County, Texas, February 23, 1855. Worked for the Millet ranching interests in the Clear Fork area from September 1876 to June 1877, when he joined the Rangers. Investigated the Larn killing. Gave a detailed account to historian J.R. Webb on March 15, 1947, when he was 92.

POE, JOHN WILLIAM: Lawman, buffalo hunter, vigilante. May have been a party to the Larn killing. Born in Kentucky. Arrived in Fort Griffin in 1872. Later went to New Mexico, and became a rancher and banker. Died in New Mexico in July 1923.

VAN RIPER, J.E.: Texas Ranger during the Larn Affair. Acting commander of Company B in Campbell's absence.

Gunslingers

BLAND, BILL: Foreman for the Millet outfit, and associate of John Larn and John Selman. Killed in a gunfight at Donley & Carroll's Saloon in January 1877.

LARN, JOHN M.: Second sheriff of Shackelford County, and considered one of the best. Cattleman, cattle thief and killer. Born, March 1, 1849, apparently in Mobile, Alabama. Married Mary Jane Mathews, daughter of Joseph Beck Mathews and Caroline Spears. Sworn in as sheriff, April 22, 1876. Submitted resignation March 7, 1877. Gunned down in the Albany Jail, June 24, 1878.

SELMAN, JOHN HENRY: Born, Madison County, Arkansas, November 16, 1839. Notorious gunman and reprobate in the Fort Griffin area. Died of gunshot wounds in El Paso, April 6, 1896.

Soiled Doves

DENO, LOTTIE: Woman of mystery. Lover of John Shannessy and Johnny Golden. Left Fort Griffin after Shannessy had Golden killed.

GAMBEL, INDIAN KATE: Fort Griffin prostitute who sheltered desperadoes and renegades.

MCCABE, MOLLIE: Operated Palace of Beautiful Sin.

MARTIN, HURRICANE MINNIE: Wife of Hurricane Bill Martin and lover of John Selman.

Interested Parties

BIGGERS, DON: Author, wrote *Shackelford County Sketches*, a history of the area.

BLAIR, DAVE: Trail agent, representing Fort Worth interests.

CLARKE, A.A.: Attorney and civic leader, Shackelford County. Lived in Albany.

EARP, WYATT: Deputy marshal from Dodge City, Kansas. Claimed he met Doc Holiday in Fort Griffin.

GARRETT, PATRICK FLOYD (PAT): Buffalo hunter at Fort Griffin in 1876. Later became a lawman in New Mexico and killed Billy the Kid.

GOLDEN, JOHNNY: Lottie Deno's lover. Murdered at instigation of Johnny Shannessy.

GRANT, BEN O.: Scholar. Wrote a thesis, *Early History of Shackleford County*, interviewing many pioneers.

HAVERTY, PETE: Fort Griffin livery stable owner and horse racer.

HAYES, BILL: Rancher and former employer of John Larn. Mobbed at Larn's instigation in 1873.

HOLLIDAY, JOHN HENRY, D.D.S. (DOC HOLLIDAY): Tubercular gambler and friend of Wyatt Earp. Arrested in Fort Griffin in 1875.

JEFFRIES, (JEFFRESS), WILLIAM: County attorney for Shackelford County. Badly wounded in the gunfight at Donley & Carroll's.

LARN, WILL: John and Mary Larn's son.

LEDBETTER, W.H.: Operated a salt works in Shackelford County.

LYNCH, L.C.: Area rancher and judge.

MARTIN, HURRICANE BILL: Fort Griffin badman and reprobate.

MILLET, ALONZO: Rancher in Throckmorton County.

NEIGHBORS, ROBERT SIMPSON: Superintendent of the Brazos Indian agencies. Assassinated in 1859.

POE, SOPHIE A.: John William Poe's wife and biographer, wrote *Buckboard Days*.

SHANNESSY, JOHN (DICK SHANNESSY): Saloon keeper in Fort Griffin. Lottie Deno's lover. Arranged murder of Johnny Golden.

STRIBLING, C.K.: Shackelford County political and civic leader.

WOOSLEY, ED and FRANK: James Brock's cousins who fabricated a murder and tried to frame him for it.

WRAY, JOHN W.: John Larn's attorney.

Bibliography
and Index

Bibliography

GOVERNMENT DOCUMENTS

Claims for Spoliations Committed by Indians and Mexicans (To accompany Bill H.R. 728), House of Reps. Report No. 535, 36th Cong., 1st Sess., May 18, 1860.

Post Medical Report, Fort Griffin, Texas, 1867-1881, microfilm copy, Arnulfo Oliveira Mem. Lib., Fort Brown, Brownsville, TX.

Shackelford County, Justice of the Peace Court, Precinct 1, Cause No. 26, The State of Texas vs. John Selman, John M. Larn, Thomas Curtis, Thomas Selman, _____. Thistle and Jimmy Herrington, June 1878, electrostatic copies in Old Jail Art Center and Archive, Albany, TX.

Shackelford County Minutes of the Dist. Court Vol. A, 6-7-[18]75 to 3-1-[18]84, Dist. Clerk's Office, Shackelford Co. Courthouse, Albany, TX.

State of Texas, Office of the Adjutant General, Annual Report of the AGO, Fiscal Year Ending Aug. 31, 1878, Austin.

State of Texas, Office of the Adjutant General, Record Group 401-1159, Ranger Force, Frontier Battalion, Letters, 1878, Archives Div., Texas State Library.

Texas Travel Handbook. Austin: Dept. of Highways and Public Trans., n.d. (1986).

MANUSCRIPT SOURCES

J. Evetts Haley File. Panhandle-Plains Hist. Soc., Canyon, TX.

James Will Myers Papers. Panhandle-Plains Hist. Soc.

Robert Nail Papers. Old Jail Art Center and Archive, Albany.

H.C. Smith Papers. Panhandle-Plains Hist. Soc.

Earl Vandale Collection. Barker Texas History Center, Univ. of TX, Austin.

J.R. Webb Papers. Rupert N. Richardson Research Center, Hardin-Simmons Univ., Abilene, TX.

Unpublished Theses

Grant, Ben O. "Early History of Shackelford County." MA thesis, Hardin-Simmons Univ., Abilene, TX, June 1936.
Skaggs, Jimmy M. "The Great Western Cattle Trail to Dodge City, Kansas." MA thesis, Texas Tech. Coll., Lubbock, Aug. 1965.

Newspapers

Albany *News*   Fort Worth *Democrat*
Dallas *News*   Galveston *News*
Fort Griffin *Echo*   Jacksboro *Frontier Echo*

Articles

Crimmins, M.L., ed. "Col. J.K.F. Mansfield's Report of the Inspection of the Department of Texas in 1856." *SWHQ*, Vol. 42, No. 4, Apr. 1939.
Gard, Wayne. "How They Killed the Buffalo." *American Heritage*, Vol. 7, No. 5, Aug. 1956.
Holden, W.C. "Frontier Journalism." *SWHQ*, Vol. 32, No. 3, Jan. 1929.
_____. "Law and Lawlessness on the Texas Frontier, 1876-1890." *SWHQ*, Vol. 44, No. 2, Oct. 1940.
Rister, C.C. "Documents Relating to General W.T. Sherman Southern Plains Indian Policy, 1871-1875." *Panhandle-Plains Historical Review*, Vol. 9, 1936.
_____. "The Significance of the Destruction of the Buffalo in the Southwest." *SWHQ* Vol. 33, No. 1, July 1929.
Webb, J.R. The various magazine articles by J.R. Webb were consulted in their original manuscript form in the J.R. Webb Papers (which see) and are cited as such.
Webber, Gale, supervising ed. "Buffalo Guns in Texas: The Sharps Rifle Company Texas Letters, 1875-1882." *The Museum Journal* 12, 1970, West Texas Museum Assoc., Texas Tech. Univ., Lubbock.

FILM

Sturges, John (director). *Gunfight at the O.K. Corral*, Paramount, 1957.

BOOKS

Biggers, Don H. *Shackelford County Sketches*. Edited and Annotated by Joan Farmer. Albany and Fort Griffin: The Clear Fork Press, 1974.

Butler, Ann M. *Daughters of Joy, Sisters of Misery: Prostitutes in the American West, 1865-1890*. Urbana and Chicago: Univ. of Illinois Press, 1985.

Dobie, J. Frank. *A Vaquero of the Brush Country*. Austin: Univ. of Texas Press, 1981.

Gard, Wayne. *The Chisholm Trail*. Norman: Univ. of Oklahoma Press, 1954.

_____. *Frontier Justice*. Norman: Univ. of Oklahoma Press, 1981.

_____. *The Great Buffalo Hunt*. Lincoln: Univ. of Nebraska Press, 1968.

Haley, James L. *The Buffalo War: The History of the Red River Indian Uprising of 1874*. Norman: Univ. of Oklahoma Press, 1985.

_____. *Texas, An Album of History*. Garden City, N.Y.: Doubleday and Co., 1985.

Hart, Herbert M. *Old Forts of the Southwest*. Seattle: Superior Publishing Co., 1964.

Holden, Frances Mayhugh. *Lambshead Before Interwoven: A Texas Range Chronicle, 1848-1878*. College Station, Texas: A&M Univ. Press, 1982.

Hunter, J. Marvin. *The Trail Drivers of Texas*. Austin: Univ. of Texas Press, 1985.

Jahns, Pat. *The Frontier World of Doc Holliday: Faro Dealer from Dallas to Deadwood*. Lincoln: Univ. of Nebraska Press, 1979.

Lake, Stuart N. *Wyatt Earp, Frontier Marshal*. Boston and N.Y.: Houghton Mifflin Co., 1931.

Leckie, William H.. *The Military Conquest of the Southern Plains*. Norman: Univ. of Oklahoma Press, 1963.

Ledbetter, Barbara A. Neal. *Fort Belknap, Frontier Saga*. Burnet, Texas: Eakin Press, 1982.

Matthews (Mathews), Sallie Reynolds. *Interwoven: A Pioneer Chronicle.* College Station: Texas A&M Univ. Press, 1982.

McConnell, H.H. *Five Years a Cavalryman.* Jacksboro: J.N. Rodgers and Co., 1889.

Metz, Leon C[laire]. *Pat Garrett, The Story of a Western Lawman.* Norman: Univ. of Oklahoma Press, 1973.

_____. *John Selman, Gunfighter.* Norman: Univ. of Oklahoma Press, 1980.

Myers, John Myers. *Doc Holliday.* Lincoln: Univ. of Nebraska Press, 1973.

Poe, Sophie A. *Buckboard Days.* Albuquerque: Univ. of New Mexico Press, 1981.

Ramsdell, Charles William. *Reconstruction in Texas.* Austin: Univ. of Texas Press, 1970.

Rathjen, Frederick W. *The Texas Panhandle Frontier.* Austin: Univ. of Texas Press, 1985.

Richards, Norman V. *Cowboy Movies.* New York: Gallery Books, 1984.

Rister, Carl Coke. *Fort Griffin on the Texas Frontier.* Norman: Univ. of Oklahoma Press, 1986.

Robinson, Charles M. III. *Frontier Forts of Texas.* Houston: Gulf Publishing Co., 1986.

Rye, Edgar, *The Quirt and the Spur: Vanishing Shadows of the Texas Frontier.* Chicago: W.B. Conkey Co., 1909.

Skaggs, Jimmy M. *The Cattle-Trailing Industry: Between Supply and Demand, 1866-1890.* Lawrence: Univ. of Kansas Press, 1973.

Sonnichsen, C.L. *I'll Die Before I'll Run: The Story of the Great Feuds of Texas.* New York: The Devin-Adair Co., 1962.

Smithwick, Noah. *The Evolution of a State or Recollections of Old Texas Days.* Austin: Univ. of Texas Press, 1983.

Thomason, John W. *Lone Star Preacher.* New York: Charles Scribner's Son, 1941.

Turner, Alford E., ed. *The Earps Talk.* College Station, Texas: Creative Publishing Co., 1980.

Webb, Walter Prescott. *The Texas Rangers: A Century of Frontier Defense.* Austin: Univ. of Texas Press, 1965.

Wheeler, Keith, and editors of Time-Life Books: *The Old West: The Townsmen.* New York: Time-Life Books, 1975.

Index

The Frontier World of Fort Griffin by Charles Robinson III has been designed by and produced under the direction of Robert A. Clark. It was typeset in Palatino by Prosperity Press, Spokane, Washington. It was bound and printed by Thompson-Shore, Inc. of Dexter, Michigan.